THE WOMAN WHO NO LONGER KNOWS

THE WOMAN WHO NO LONGER KNOWS

An A to Z of the changing relationship
between men and women

ANNIE WILSON

ROWAN COMMUNICATIONS LIMITED

First published in the UK in 1998 by Rowan Communications Ltd.
Fourways, Chalford, Westbury, Wilts, BA13 3RE
Fax: (01373) 827988

Printed by Whitstable Litho Printers, Whitstable, Kent

ISBN: 1 902183 02 9

A catalogue record of this book is available from the British Library

Contents

Introduction

This book is a channelled book. The word 'channel' today refers to a vast spectrum of experience, but for me the journey is a spiritual unfolding, not an attempt to harness psychic abilities. The aim is to achieve the inner integration of spirit and matter, to allow us to operate out of the limitless vistas of Soul consciousness.

I like to think of the channelling work I do as a by-product of this journey, which has taken twenty-five years or more so far. This particular way of 'accessing information' could not have manifest until these explorations, often painful, had taken place. The guides describe the mechanism as 'encompassing more of the universal mind'.

I do not feel comfortable naming guides, but prefer to have an explanation that suits me and resonates with the way I feel about things. With all the scrutiny I can muster I trust the source to be from the highest realms of Light. The guides offer tough love to be sure, but always with humour. These beings want us to move forward, not only for ourselves but for planet Earth and beyond.

My journey has been the 'feminine journey'. My first book 'The Wise Virgin' was the result of several years' experience towards an awareness of the spiritual aspect of the feminine and the link to the 'direct knowing' of the Higher Self. The second phase was the difficult and dark 'descent'; an awakening to the body and to the Earth. This has led to what I call the inner marriage of the masculine and feminine aspects of womanhood, and the awareness of the Soul as mediator between Heaven and Earth, spirit and matter, through the human heart.

And yet, I have always felt that the real purpose of the feminine journey was to herald the imminent emergence of a new male energy on planet Earth, symbolised by the promise of the return of Arthur, the once and future king. And now, my work with clients – solicitors, doctors, social workers among them – is bringing a clutch of men, many of whom were previously unaware of a spiritual quest, who recognise that their lives are changing, and that they are no longer who they thought they were.

The guides are showing them a new perception of themselves, and of Earth, which is really exciting. They are also finding out that it is not an easy path. They, too, are in a descent and having to look at their unconscious patterns 'on the way down'.

Although, of course, not all these men are in relationships, there is a remarkable unfolding in the coming together of what I call 'women of consciousness', or as the guides call them the 'women in white', with these new 'Earth Men'. And as they find a truer sense of themselves, a new relationship can develop between men and women, which the guides call 'Dyadic Partnership'.

For me there is no point in writing something that I do not know in my own experience. Along my line towards the new male energy came the man who is now my second husband, Martin. In this book the guides say that these new relationships are about 'cherishing and challenging'. It is also true that to understand what is going on in the psyche of the collective, you have to live it. On both counts we have been challenged enough and have weathered storms enough to last a lifetime.

For ten years Martin specialised in making television programmes on disability. His interest in matters more esoteric – particularly on the relevance of past lives to our understanding of the life we lead now – began many years ago. There is no doubt that we are 'meant' to be together but I give Martin credit for making it plain to me!

It was he who pronounced that we should work as well as live together, but I suspect he might have been more circumspect if he had known what that work would entail. I salute Martin's courage in looking at the difficult material within his own and the collective male psyche, and my courage for sticking with it! Men, it seems, are having to look at issues of sexuality, rage and violence in a far more gruelling way than women – although all inner work is challenging.

I have worked with Martin in exactly the same way as I work with clients, but far more intensively. The guides use guided imagery techniques to channel the experience that the client most needs in order to understand and release negative patterns. Their aim, above all, is to lead a person into their 'magnificence', their full creative potential. This can effect change in the body as well as the psyche.

Martin and I have both struggled and fought against our changing roles and the sacrifices that have been necessary on both sides to move through to the greater rewards of this new adventure called 'interdependence'.

In our work with the guides it was they who suggested that the 'A-Z' should be written. In fact, the course of this book frequently mirrors our own journey through the period of writing. As I channel, fully present, Martin is able to perceive and experience, often symbolically, information that he could not possibly access in any other way. (In his dialogue with the guides, Martin's responses are highlighted in italics.)

We offer our book in good faith.

A for Answer

There is no shame, no blame about understanding the answer before you understand the question. It's a matter of creating the means to understand the question if the answer becomes apparent. Remember the Grail story? The answer <u>was</u> in the question, wasn't it? And yet the question "Whom does the grail serve?" was never quite understood. So in our view there needs to be an answer first, which is about really resonating with the way the planet is going now. There is a most incredible shift going on, in the sense of a real change in the relationship between Heaven and Earth on Earth.

In past eras a very dark shadow passed over the Earth and in our view this shadow was a deeply disastrous event for planet Earth. It took away the planet's self-motivational field in a way that created distance between the old Heaven and a more realistic way of becoming related to Earth consciousness. There was such a darkness over the Earth that all people in the incarnating process were made to feel unworthy in some way.

Now, however, this sense of unworthiness is being realigned within each individual, so that now every human being can recognise their own value in the scheme of things. And if you think about it, how incredible would be the shift if all people knew things they have never, ever known, that no one on planet Earth has ever known before about the human being. It is quite a challenge to perceive that every human being has access within himself (or, of course, herself) to information that would change the entire nature of humanity on Earth.

That is the prospect we offer in this book. If every human being is more than they can ever imagine themselves to be, then of course men and women are the repositories of this information. Who else is there to be guardian of this way of being human in the magnificent form we speak of? And if men and women are reposi tories of their own 'new beingness', then clearly men and women will be very different creatures to the ones they have been before.

May we suggest to the reader that at our level of manifestation we are unable to tell the difference between men and women. It is only as the lines become more dense that the distinction between men and women on planet Earth is apparent.

We must make the distinction between our relationship to the cosmos and planet Earth's relation to the cosmos. We are an energetic marker point in the cosmos in such a way that we feel ourselves to manifest a more refined level of resonance than Earth manifests in the cosmos.

In this sense we make ourselves more manifestly resonant to human beings than the still more refined energetic manifestations in the universe. In other words, we are a mediating point between the finer levels and the denser levels and this is why we are releasing this information at this time. There is a need for the denser levels of energy in the cosmos to refine more and more as the universe progresses.

In our view, then, men and women on planet Earth are refining their energetic resonance. They need to become more and more refined in themselves in order to release the denser energies into the Earth repository and make themselves the mediators between the finer levels of cosmic resonance and denser matter of Earth itself.

The reason men in particular need now to become more resonant with Earth consciousness, is that men will eventually become the leaders of a more markedly resonant relationship between Heaven, Mankind and Earth. There will be a new relationship between the finer levels of cosmic resonance and Earth itself, which is becoming in its own right a resonant conscious being. We suggest that eventually the male human being will be the mediator between Heaven and Earth in such a way that men will become more able to lead the way into a very different resonance on planet Earth.

So, men are to be the new leaders in a changing world. And in our view, that means a great shift within men and women. Of course, in some ways this is already taking place. But many people who are recognising the shifts in the energetic field, are totally unable to understand what is going on – not only inside themselves, but also within their partners. There is likely to be a sense of chaos when the reality of the changing energies becomes more apparent in the coming years. So there needs to be a real understanding of the way men and women are becoming more and more refined within themselves but cannot yet recognise what that means and how it will affect them, and the rest of humanity, as it continues to move forward.

The inner being is changing beyond measure now. There will be more and more opportunities to make these changes in a more or less painless way, unless someone is so reluctant to recognise the changing nature of things that they are 'hit over the head' in a way that makes it more uncomfortable than it need be.

We feel many people have begun to accept that life is changing, but there needs to be a real understanding of what these changes are doing inside the male particularly. There is a deep destabilisation happening inside men right now, felt by many men as a shift in the aggressive forces within them. These forces are actually heightening now, because it's time to release this aggression and manifest the energy as a creative force for change, rather than as a mammoth release of tension that is beyond their ability to cope with.

In fact, this tension manifest inside men at this time, is the tension of the Earth itself, in some way. There needs to be an explosion of the tension as a creative passion, if you like, rather than the current mood of aggressive, violent behaviour which is inside most men – if they were to be honest about it. May we suggest the answer, then, is in the release by men of the aggressive forces within the Earth. These need to be released now, if human beings are to become finer in themselves and to realign, in a strategic way, to the unfolding cosmic purpose on Earth.

We trust that our words will resonate with your own lives right now. In our view the answer to the question is that more and more people are realising their true worth in some way, and in that recognition they are seeing themselves as human beings for the first time in their lives. But, until the male on planet Earth has done the task of releasing his aggression, the Earth cannot refine in the way it is destined to do.

May we ask the reader to make the leap of faith that if what we say is true, then there is a task that women too must perform in the scheme of things. Women must release from within themselves 'the warrior', who is no longer appropriate if the male is to achieve his task of releasing the rage of the Earth.

We see the woman in the planetary sense now, as the receiver of the manifestly changing energies of refined resonance. In this regard she needs now to become a 'repository of energy', and as such her whole relationship to herself needs to change profoundly. We see women taking the opportunity to serve the male in a very new way because, as we see it, the woman is able to change to become the new woman more easily than men are able to release their rage – which we perceive to be resonant with their more masculine approach to life.

In other words, it is women who must first become aware, in order for men to do their task. Women, then, will mediate their consciousness to the men in a watered down form so that men can continue the task of refinement on Earth.

The Grail is a feminine concept of renewal and receptivity which now becomes the servant of the Grail king – the male. Women will serve men, and men will become their own masters of destiny. Men will become aware that the Earth is ready to speak to the human race, in order that humanity may refine and move forward.

*   *   *

"We feel Martin is in the woods. The woods will make Martin feel so safe that the trees begin to open the way for him to become deeply immersed in the ways of the woods. Martin will feel so safe that the trees begin to feel the only safety he has in the world, because the way that life is evolving makes the world feel very unsafe.

"How is the world evolving that makes men feel unsafe, Martin?

Ask the trees. What is happening to scare men in the world? First of all, why do the trees care that men are feeling unsafe in the world?"

"The trees have a vested interest. Their security is bound up with the plight of the masculine. Men have, in effect, become castrated, powerless, rendered inept, because women, in seeking balance – which nobody denies was due – have gone on to overtake males and presume on their role. The well-being of the planet depends on balance between men and women; it's as simple as that."

"What do the trees feel about the plight of men, right now?"

"In earlier times the trees felt safe with humanity. The well-being of the human was tied up with the well-being of the planet, and so of the trees themselves. The trees are aghast that this change in balance has led to male aggression against planetary resources.

"Men are now taking it out on the planet because of their frustration and anger in the usurpation of their divine right to be Earth Men; the understanders of the planet, toilers of the soil, in tune with the juices of the planet.

"Why is it necessary that the Earth has become this desperate though? We feel women had to become conscious, didn't they? Tell us what happens when a woman comes into the wood."

"It feels, although she walks in innocence, that there is great fear from the trees. The trees shrivel. They are almost victims of the drama. The planet has to suffer for a scripted drama, the play's already written."

"The drama required the planet to suffer?"

"Planet Earth set up the blueprint whereby human beings came in innocence to the planet, and in innocence lived lightly on the Earth.

They understood in lightness the way the planet operated, the flow of nature, yin and yang, leylines; in tune with the Garden of Eden. They were idyllic times."

"But into the blueprint of Earth was also written that women should descend from innocence to become conscious, so that men have felt deeply threatened, and their natural role of provider and protector has been undermined. The only way now for the man to be successful in his own eyes is to go and be macho, which he cannot do with the women. So now he rapes the planet.

"This descent is not a recent event. The pain of the descent of women started with the French Revolution. Before that, in the 1700's, novels by authors such as Jane Austen – now interestingly in vogue – showed that men were men and women were women. Looking at the writing of the period, the French revolution was the first time women were treated as equal, although soon afterwards men realised the enormity of the situation, that they had opened a can of worms.

"Other revolutions had the same precept of equality. What happened in Russia was the opening up of a more egalitarian mood in which the slave mentality was blown apart. Revolutions enabled women to get out from under their slavery to male dominance. The stress of the trees, however, is connected to the slave mentality now being visited on men, isn't it Martin?"

"I see the image of a tree used to whip a man. Men are the whipping boys of the women and the trees are caught up in that because inevitably male aggression leads to their destruction."

"What do men feel slave to right now?"

"Slave to the wind of change; a force that they cannot resist. They are shackled by the mind-set they have, which is forced on them by the attitude of the women who simply wish to control their

maleness. I see vampish women walking down a catwalk and pushing down a line of men into the water. The audience is screaming, excited. Men are powerless. Their beauty and minds are ignored – a sort of reverse of the way men treated women."

"The women have become predatory, bound by the zeitgeist. You can move so much within the zeitgeist but you cannot change the spirit of the age. It is still written.

"How do male politicians work now?"

"The trees show them in a circle talking to each other, colluding. They say anything as long as it's placating and will work for the time being. They are too fearful to confront; it's too dangerous to step out of line."

"Whom does the Grail serve? Whom does the feminine serve? What do the trees say in answer to the question?"

"The Grail serves the gentle oscillation, the balance between male and female."

"At this moment, where is the balance best served?"

"The trees are bent over backwards in enormous tension. The sun – a male sun – is a tree tied back, aghast. It symbolises men as speechless. They are bound by what has been done. Balance is to release tension, to allow the male principle to flow backwards and forwards with the female. It is excruciating at the deepest level. But as two trees move with the wind, as the wind changes backwards and forwards, there is harmony."

B for Breath

We feel the releasing of breath is the most significant thing that each individual on the planet does for himself, and for the Universe. It is a really valuable way in which the Universe is kept in touch with what we like to call the Earth's business of being a planet of love. Perhaps it is hard to believe in this day and age, but Earth is indeed the planet of love.

It is love that keeps the Universe turning and growing and becoming in the way it does and shall do evermore. It was God's plan that Earth should become the planet that made the world of man the cosmic regulator, if you like, and in that regulating of the cosmos, love would be the ruling energy in the relationship between Heaven, Earth and Man.

There is no one on this planet who cannot live a life of compassionate lovingness. It is the destiny of man to become a being of loving kindness. It is the journey of humankind to remember God's Compassionate Will, in the sense of becoming God on Earth. It is the destiny of human beings to become God on Earth, because Earth is God's love incarnate.

Feel that deeply in your being now. It is important to recognise the truth of God's love incarnate on Earth as the destiny of mankind, especially when there is so much apparent antithesis of love on Earth. More apparent than love is violent rage, isn't it? And violent rage is, in fact, the outpouring of Earth's rage against man for being the repository of God's love, believe it or not.

Earth could not bear man to be the repository of God's love because Earth herself is not that loving. In her unconscious state she is ruthless in tooth and claw – which is why the 'selfish gene' was so successful. Indeed it is Earth's wish to perpetuate her own kind that has created the rage, now that man is beginning to recognise himself as the son of God as well as the daughter of man.

There will be shifts and changes in distressing ways, as we have already seen, as the Earth releases her rage through the male being on Earth. In fact, men have a far deeper relationship to Earth than women, paradoxically, and it is male rage that is perpetually in vision at this moment, not the loving Earth. True maleness will emerge once Earth releases her rage at being home to the sons of God who carry within them the spiritual gene of loving kindness and compassion.

May we suggest the Earth herself is breathing fire and brimstone at the shifts taking place in her consciousness right now. As more and more people recognise their inner spiritual selves, they are releasing the Earth's rage in some way and releasing her cloying, jealous need to stay in control of the human beings on her surface. Eventually there will be that Golden Age everyone speaks of, in which all men and women will have let go their raging, in order to allow in the loving God within. They will resonate to that Love of God that all religions speak of, but very few fully understand.

The most important aspect of the human being is his ability to breathe in God's love and allow it to circulate around him. Then to breathe out all the negativity within him, down into the ground where the Earth herself composts it, to be recycled into some glorious manna from Heaven again.

There is a cyclical relationship between Heaven and Earth. If the human being can breathe in God's love and release the negative material stacked inside him, into the Earth's compost heap, he helps to release the Earth's rage and negativity. This is complementary to discovering the negativity within himself in a more therapeutic way.

Breathing, then, is importantly a most efficacious way of helping the Earth right now. Breathing well, in and out, down and round, in a very conscious manner. This is something the yogis have known since time immemorial, and indeed yoga is a wonderful practice because it does just as we have said. It cleans out the body and pours the negative staleness into the Earth's compost heap, allowing a circulation of energy through the body. More energy can be breathed in from the ultimate source, the Will of God, which enables the rest of the cosmos to feel the loving energy.

Like a satellite bounces energy back to Earth, Earth bounces the Love of God back to the Universe and life moves forward.

May we suggest you contemplate this extraordinary sense of the Love of God being bounced back from Earth to the Universe through the breath of mankind. Not something to be taken lightly, we feel.

Indeed, no one breathes really well, simply because, except for the yogis, man doesn't fully understand how important breath is. And of course there are karmic reasons why the breath is so poorly executed. We have said already that man is determined to feel unworthy, and unworthiness actually causes shortened breath. We suggest the reason why asthmatics have such difficulty catching their breath is because unworthiness lies in their personal and family history. There is a karmic predisposition to feel unworthy and this life is a journey towards self-worth.

It is not simple to describe how breath is so important, but in our view, although ostensibly more and more people are finding breathing difficult because of the increased toxic outpouring of industrial life, the deeper reason is that many individuals are now incarnating to understand the pernicious nature of lack of self-worth. The task is to become aware of who you truly are.

*   *   *

"We feel Martin is able to feel the catch in his breath right now. How does it feel to have a catch in the breath?"

"It seems like a constant reminder of something not right."

"It feels like a reminder, doesn't it? We feel Martin will feel the catch of the breath inside his solar plexus now. The feeling of something being not quite right is stronger there. What is not quite right, suddenly?"

"I keep seeing walls – something denied. Tall, stone walls with castellation that can't be accessed because they are so heavily

defended. Inside the wall I feel inert. There is no feeling; it's absolutely dense. I feel myself turning inward, with no interest in the external, only to look inside the fortification. Inside the fortification I can see ritual dances and movement; flags. I'm totally oblivious to any outside stimulus."

"The wall holds in the Warrior Queen, doesn't it?"

"There's a constant sense of war, of aggression. Every situation has to be dealt with by aggression, by attack, by the armed strike of the army. There is no sense of peace within the fortification and on the battlements. Such lookouts as there are only see attack, which seems to hark back to the warrior woman."

"Absolutely. How does breath come into the suggestion that the Warrior Queen is defending against aggression?"

"The sense I have in this scenario is that the prevailing attitude is Taoist, which would raise the breath to many different levels. An attack would be received in a different way, perhaps it would be a going-with-the-flow of an attack; letting the attack expend itself before addressing it; allowing its full force before the counter-attack; an understanding of the flow of any movement, as evinced by breath."

"Absolutely. So we feel Martin is able to feel attack on the breath. The breath makes Martin feel like attacking in some way."

"I'm quite resistant to that."

"Go on. Feel the resistance to breathing attack. Feel attack is the outbreath; a blowing wind of change."

"I want to breathe in, not out, and meditate and be peaceful."

"How does that work?"

"I want to meditate, to take in the energy of the breath, prana. I sense attack is blowing forth air, aggression. It is not listening to the stillness around."

"Why does Martin want to breathe in against the Warrior Queen suddenly?"

"I see the warring of the Warrior Queen. But I see no purpose to it."

"Why no purpose?"

"We have a stunning land; an ordered society; fine craft and culture. We live an idyllic existence, but there is something within her which demands obedience from others. Above all, to attack and suppress others."

"We feel Martin will be able to feel into the Warrior Queen now, who is under attack in the situation."

"She is greatly feared because she is liable to strike out at any time, for any reason."

"But we feel her point of view. What is she defending in her view?"

"Defending territory."

"But more than that."

"Her children. Her people."

"Absolutely. But more than that."

"Her integrity. Her being is threatened."

"Why threatened?"

"Because she's a woman."

"Absolutely. She's a woman above all, isn't she? How does she feel as a woman in this situation?"

"A mixture. She sneers at the weakness of men. In her view they are incompetent, lack initiative and brains."

"Go on. What else are men incapable of in this situation?"

"A connection with God that she has. An in-touchness."

"Absolutely. The 'in-touchness' she has with God. The Warrior Queen knows God in some way. How does she know God?"

"She senses God in her being. She is in touch with Earth as well. They are one and the same."

"Why?"

"I have an image of bleeding into the Earth. Fertility. As a male I cannot understand."

"We wish Martin to continue in this vein about the blood. What does bleeding give women that men can't have?"

"There is an enormous sense of lineage inherent in women, the continuing power of the blood. Being the living repository of the living blueprint."

"Absolutely. But also the breath now. What is there in the breath that men can't have?"

"A woman's closeness to the planet in all aspects of her body. Sensitivity to the breath."

"We feel Martin is able to say more about the breath."

"I see nipples, breasts."

"What does breath create in the breasts, Martin?"

"Energy to nurture future generations."

"The breath holds the blueprint which the nipples pass on in some way, don't they?"

"We feel Martin can sum up the reason why women are becoming the Warrior Queen against men."

"The feeling I have is that as men become marginalised by the progress of women, the whole dynamic is exacerbated. A super breed of warrior women is created who are so fed up with the dynamic with men that they go even further in their war-like stance. The end result is one of annihilation for men. A noted reduction in the sperm count questions their relevance in today's society and creates a lack of confidence in their ability to find any function."

"Now, we feel Martin is able to remember the statue of Joan of Arc in Aix-en-Provence. We suggest Martin is able to feel her making herself more motivated to become the Rainbow Warrior. Tell us why she can now be less derogatory about men, and therefore softer in her warrior phase."

"Originally the circumstances were such that there was no alternative. The country needed leadership and Joan of Arc was the right man for the job, so to speak. The principle stuck and has got stuck, and come what may a softening is necessary because the warrior principle will destroy society. Joan of Arc took up arms because it was necessary to save what she loved. Now it is necessary to mitigate her war-like nature, again to protect the society she loves."

"What is required for the woman, for example, to let go the Warrior Queen? Feel Annie's breath as a child when she was an asthmatic. What was happening?"

"Fear of drawing in a full breath and of the consequences of drawing in a full breath, of life-giving entry."

"Why was she afraid of the breath that breathes life into her?"

"Fear of being overtaken by it. Also fear of being unworthy of it."

"What does that unworthiness create in the woman in terms of the Warrior Queen syndrome?"

"To strike out. I've gone full circle, to a heavily defended space. A defence of the situation, the rationale for being a Warrior Queen. It's the Warrior Queen's greatest fear to surrender."

"Surrender to life. Why is this so terrible?"

"To lose control is frightening."

"Absolutely. And in terms of the male right now?"

"The sense of surrender to a weak, inept male is somehow unworthy for the grand Warrior Queen. Simply not good enough."

"But if she takes in the breath now, we feel something strange happens, doesn't it?"

"The breath says it's not a surrender anymore."

"Why not?"

"Because if the Warrior Queen puts down her sword for a moment, she realises it's a coming together of equals. A balance

is struck. It is now time to participate in an equal and opposite relationship."

"Absolutely. We feel the Warrior Queen feels less fearful now, doesn't she? Why?"

"She sees she has been looking through a dark glass at the situation and now sees the wall is crumbling."

"Absolutely. The wall is crumbling, isn't it? So what happens when the wall crumbles?"

"Rejoicing. Peace prevails. Creativity can return to relationship."

"Why will it return?"

"Women don't need to humiliate men any more, so there can be a bonding energetically. A circular energy, a spiral."

"And men?"

"A million men going 'phew....' in great relief."

"And when the relief is there?"

"Men are fearful because deep down they know the blueprint for the next phase. It will be difficult, their descent, to look at their darkest unconscious shadow material. But it might give women an incentive to know they are not giving up something they hold dear for nothing!"

C for Communication

Communication with partners is never easy, is it? Communication means recognising difference. Communication is the real problem in partnership, as indeed it is in all relationships, but in partnership particularly. Each partner comes into play in so many different ways when they are in communication with each other as man and woman in depth.

We feel many partnerships find communication difficult. It is not easy to be making love one minute and making war the next, which is often the way it feels. If communication is good, then war breaks out more often than would seem desirable. And if communication is not good then war becomes the means by which one person fights the other, but it isn't expressed. There is an atmosphere in the relationship and strife within both partners, not just the one who sees himself at war with the other. There is a natural order of war inside men and women, right now, which needs to be released if men and women are to become compatible together in the way they can be and will be in future.

Men and women are at war because there is, in the system as it were, such a war-like feeling between the mother and the male child that there will also always be war inside men and women towards each other, however much they love each other. There will always be strife inside, even if not apparent in communication.

Those who believe they are not at war with their other half are deluding themselves into dependency; into 'becoming the other' in such a way that it doesn't feel like war inside. In fact, what is happening in this event is that the dependency is creating sameness from one person to the other. The partner who is able to depend on the other makes him or herself subservient to the other's needs, and then there is no war.

This can be the easy option, sometimes, and that is why there is often such one-sidedness in a relationship. One partner is 'powering over' the other to such an extent that they are totally subsumed. It happens more often than people might imagine. But, in a more balanced relationship, there is war between the male and female partners at some more or less conscious level.

It is not easy to be a partner and we don't blame those who give up on relationship because it is too difficult. Indeed, those who are coming together now to realise a new level of Dyadic Partnership – as we like to call it – are ironically those who are having the most difficulty. Those who are destined to understand the new dyadic partnership will in fact, en route, feel even more at war than others who have, if you like, accommodated partnership more independently.

May we suggest that in the coming months and years there will be almost more difficulty in making sense of relationship, as partnership becomes more and more dyadic. So what is the answer for realising relationship in a very different way?

We feel communication is the first step, because until partners can talk to each other, no one will know how it is for the other person. Many partnerships don't communicate at all. Indeed, most people make war not love in the relationships they have. War is when neither party can feel into the other person's mode of expressing themselves – which invariably happens in partnership. There is no recognition of the different ways in which men and women explore life.

Communication, then, is a very important matter indeed, because at least communicating with the partner will throw up how differently each expresses themselves in their exploration through life. And this will give a backdrop for what is to become a new partnership with a different kind of communication.

Most women do not recognise the way men explore life and most men are totally incapable of seeing that women explore life differently to the way they do themselves. It is not a question of women being emotional and men being head-driven, which is the usual way of recognising the difference between men and women. In fact, men are able to 'sense' life in a different way to women, not necessarily emotionally. And women, who on the whole are emotionally-based, are not able to understand how men sense life.

It's difficult, isn't it? Men are from Mars and women from Venus, as John Gray says!

In fact, there is more to it than just men and women exploring life in different ways. Women are not trusted by men at all and although women do trust men naturally, when the distrust of women by men seeps into the system, women recognise that men are not to be trusted after all. Does that make sense? We feel women do trust men until they inevitably prove themselves to be untrustworthy. Yet men never trust women, do they? 'Mother' can't be trusted, because she isn't the mother the men want, ever.

There is a complexity of deep patterning within men and women from time immemorial and it's just the way it is. And yet, we feel there is a new dawning in relationships that will bring 'sensing' together with 'emotional feeling', so that a new, glorious and beautiful relationship between men and women will make the world itself seem a different place.

We feel many partnerships are undergoing huge change, and of course, that means divorce is very much in vogue. But we feel the way forward now is to recognise the difficulties within each partner, and be ready to allow for change, growth and exploration inside the relationship.

It is now important to trust in some way that has not been possible before. Trust is the deepest mode of communication, isn't it? But to communicate trust and be trusting of the partner is not easy because no one trusts at all these days. Indeed, that is because God doesn't feel particularly trustworthy anymore, does He? And in our view that is the baseline. God isn't trusted much anymore because male and female make themselves God to each other, and then they feel they aren't trustworthy.

*　　*　　*

"Now, let us look at communication in another way. We feel Martin is able to become aware that the most delightful shower is raining on him. A fresh shower of light rain, making a rainbow appear in the sky. What does the rainbow feel like in the showery rain, right now?"

"It feels like the breath of Heaven. Very special energy, which seems to encompass all the planes of Heaven, if you will. It produces a peculiar note on Earth. In terms of sound vibration, its frequency."

"Tell us what the note says predominantly."

"It is a feeling of joy, of bliss."

"Absolutely. The bliss is in the rainbow note, isn't it? So we feel the rainbow communicates about bliss on Earth, doesn't it? We feel Martin is able to tell us of his own method of communicating with the Earth, right now. Just this once, he can articulate how he speaks to Earth. Feel the feeling in the solar plexus and describe it, Martin."

"It's like a beam, a ray from the rainbow that comes into the ground and – I'm slightly tickled – it's the same as a little boy would pee into the ground! A watery connection to Earth is significant."

"Absolutely. Men have a watery connection to Earth, don't they? Tell us what that means in practical detail."

"A sense of ebb and flow of energy of water in Earth is felt by men."

"Absolutely. Why by men and not women, when feeling is a woman's realm?"

"I see an arid planet, a vast continent, in the same way birds can track water, so men can lead their womenfolk, their flocks, their tribe, to wherever there is water. The fundamental ingredient for life. Men need to feel water."

"So men are able to lead women to water, exclusively, it feels. May we suggest women find water but not in the same way. Does this make sense somehow?"

"I have a pain in my solar plexus."

"Go into the pain."

"I'm feeling childbirth, a pregnant feeling."

"Go on. What happens in pregnancy in terms of water?"

"It is stored within, around the child to protect it before birth. Eventually it ruptures and water discharges."

"What do the women do in the meantime to gather water?"

"I see a well."

"What does the well mean?"

"Tapping deeply into Earth for water."

"Absolutely. But now see what men do for their water."

"They go for surface water, where flocks graze. It's a question of level. High water table. Women go for subterranean water."

"Absolutely. So feeling levels are different, aren't they? But we sense there needs to be a change in the feeling levels. We feel the men are not being nourished by the feeling level they inhabit, are they? So how is communication between men and women to change in this regard?"

"In the past men followed their instincts completely. And women followed the men's lead. Now groups of men need to talk together,

to rethink, discuss, in the way women have been acknowledged to do. Men will in future do that."

"May we suggest also that men are more able to listen to women in this regard now. Why can they hear it now?"

"It's almost as if another colour of the rainbow, another note is available to them in terms of feeling and sensitivity. A yellow, which feels like a colour of communication."

"Go on. What else can women communicate to men?"

"About men's heritage, I think. And of women's experience of their descent into the depths of their being. Nothing like knowing how it is from those who have experienced it. Women with spades, digging the muck!"

"Why are men open to listening to this from women now?"

"I see a tall cliff. Many men are on the edge looking over. There's a collective group feeling of men that this is a time of transition and at times of transition one seeks a leader. I suggest the males in this collective have to look outside the group for inspiration."

"Now Martin, feel into the way women collect water from the well. How does it feel to collect so deeply right now?"

"It is a deep, deep inspiration to bring up water from such a great depth. It also offers a connection with the bowels of the Earth."

"Why?"

"The water is purified and taken into the bosom of mother Earth. Very female."

"Men are now able to drink so deeply. How are they able to change from level to level in terms of gathering water now? Why are Earth Men gathering?"

"I see a wireless transmitter with a switch for all different frequencies. Earth Men communicate on many different frequencies: with trees, plants, the Earth itself, stones. The ability to communicate is vast, with all manner of things."

"Why is this different to women's vast ability to communicate?"

"Women have the ability to receive brilliantly; they are the receptor par excellence. But now we are into the active principle of communication, where Earth Men seek out to communicate with spiders and stones."

"Absolutely. So in terms of being the woman who no longer knows, what does the woman need to concede now?"

"She loses her privileged position in terms of Earth. It's not only by having babies you can feel in touch with Earth. It is no longer true that only women are sentient beings. Their special role on Earth is not unique anymore."

"Absolutely. We feel the most important message in the book now is that women no longer hold all the cards, as it were. We feel Martin is able to understand the deeper relationship to water now, isn't he? So he is able to tell us how the new Earth male will feel about women in the future."

"As a resource!"

"May we ask Martin to re-phrase that!"

"As a creature comfort, a help mate."

"Absolutely. But be exact here. It could be upsetting."

"The Earth Man's bliss is his partner."

"That's more like it! Tell us more how he cherishes her in this way of feeling."

"It is a mutual attraction of two feeling beings; two people who own their feelings for each other and for the planet. The concern for the planet is no longer bound up with women. In a sense Mother Earth could also become Mother-Father Earth to mirror the relationship between men and women."

"Tell us how it is that the Earth Father is now able to come into being. In other words, how Earth can now become conscious of itself."

"The birthing of the Earth Father comes through acceptance of Earth Men by women."

"Absolutely. But why was it unable to happen before?"

"Mother Earth was bound up in her anger. No male principle dare approach Mother Earth in her flaming rage, in her disregard. So there was no way to approach Mother Earth."

"Tell us why the Father Principle brings consciousness (to the planet)."

"Only as the planet comes into balance in terms of Mother-Father Earth can the cooling of Earth take place. When it begins to approach balance, the Earth becomes conscious. When Earth is in a rage it can't see anything. We truly are 'cooling it'. From red to greeny blue, to coolness and balance."

D for Dreaming

'D for dreaming' is about the dream of the age. It is a dream of real relationship between men and women. It is the ideal of relationship that is the dream now. There is a need, however, to recognise that the dream is not the old dream any more. The 'idealistic' relationship between men and women is finished with the completion of the Grail myth, if you like.

The Grail myth talked of the knight in shining armour and the lady with the favour to bestow, but we feel the knight in shining armour has done, and indeed may have overdone, his time. We feel the knight in shining armour is not the new kind of man because the knight is no longer a real man; he is simply a dream lover.

The dream lover has been a man of substance, yes, but he has been a man on a quest. He has been a man who left the woman, and just about everything else, behind to go on his quest. May we suggest that in some ways 'work' has taken the place of the quest for many men. Indeed it has become the way forward for many men and women of great intellect and abilities.

However, may we suggest that work is no longer the most important aspect of life. It is a by-product of life. The most important thing in life is 'relationship between'. Work was meant to be a way of earning a living, but ultimately has become a way of leaving behind all that is important. The art of relating has been left behind as the quest for work has become the most significant thing in many people's lives.

It is most important now to realise that work is not the whole score. It needs to be seen in a new way, more in terms of a means of fulfilling oneself within. And if that is the case, the old attitudes to work will look out of place. This is the new dream, a dream of 'becoming' that does not mean leaving relationships behind, but includes relationship in its becoming the dream.

We feel the way forward now is to acknowledge that in some ways our whole relationship to life is shifting because our work ethic is changing. In our view, the way to bring back much more into life, is to let go the old idea of work as the quest. It is now time to look at Life as the quest, as a new dream to live life in a bigger, fuller way.

We need to allow a different dreaming capacity to emerge within. It is a way of perceiving life now that does not have the driven quality that work forced on us in order to earn more and more money. This new dream needs to become a dreamier dream of fulfilment, not merely of earning a living. It is a different dream now.

We feel the way to dream a dream differently is to recognise the way it has been dreamed before. The knight in shining armour was the ideal lover. He came to the woman on a white horse and once the quest was achieved they lived happily ever after. They were ideally suited – the one who was the knight in shining armour and the other who was the woman of his favour.

We feel that this image of the knight in shining armour is absolutely wrong for this age, and yet most women in their heart of hearts expect a knight to arrive on their doorstep 'one day'. They have an image of the dream lover who will sweep them off their feet. Yet no man can be expected to fulfil this dream, can they? No man can be a perfect knight in shining armour. Men are changing, too, and they cannot live up to this expectation within the psyche of women, who, in fact, have changed so much themselves that deep down they know the knight is no longer appropriate.

It is clear that difficulties in relationship are based on the fact that the knight is no longer there, and if he were, he couldn't relate to the new woman anyway. It is such a mis-match, such a confusion, and there isn't much hope unless both sides begin to dream a different dream.

So, become aware of a knight in shining armour in your imagination. Feel how that knight becomes a real man by allowing him to get off his horse and become a real man by taking off his armour. Let him sit on the ground next to the horse, which is just an ordinary horse, not a knight's horse, and allow him to become who he feels he needs to be.

Feel this inside in your reverie right now. Give yourself time to really feel it and tell yourself how this man wants to relate to his woman friend. Make it his woman friend – not his 'mother woman', who was there to approve his every daring deed and make him feel so wonderful he could continue to be a knight in shining armour. No, a woman friend who is equally in need of approval and equally wanting to make a difference in the world.

How does this knight feel now, down on the ground next to his woman friend? Very different? To both parties? We suggest there is a big difference in making a knight become a real human being and not a dream lover. The dream lover is not possible any longer, and in our view this is what needs to shift in some way, so that men and women will become friends in a different way. Lovers in the 'knight in shining armour and fair lady' ideal no longer work in any way at all.

*   *   *

"We feel D is for dreaming: daydreaming. We feel D is for releasing a dream. We feel dreaming is in the realm of possibilities which are to become realities. Dreaming is the most practical way of making something happen now. We say this because when the woman no longer knows she can dream differently.

"We feel Martin is able to become aware of a very nice dream lover inside himself. A woman who is the epitome of loving surrender, who feels the most beautiful task of all is to make the man happy.

"We feel the dream lover is a woman of great skill in doing this kind of loving. We feel her own life is so full of delight, that her man becomes the focus of that delight too. We feel the dream lover is in a way Martin's ideal shape, but not too thin. We feel the dream lover is in a white dress. We feel her making Martin a really lovely shirt. She is able to do the necessary things to make Martin feel a hundred dollars.

"We feel her really warm and sensuous in Martin's presence. We feel she needs her own counsel sometimes but feels the most delightful peace when her man is happy. We feel she is a lovely woman in every way, isn't she Martin? What is she like this dream lover?"

"She is a joy to come home to. Home is a very special place. It is a haven of joy. It is an excitement to come home because the look in her eyes is so welcoming, pools of regard, of love."

"May we suggest to Martin that he is now puts Annie in this place, not the dream lover."

"Annie has her hands on her lap. There's a small feeling of confrontation, non-acceptance. There is a different note to the dream lover who is accepting, and in that acceptance makes it all right for her man to be himself."

"Absolutely. The dream lover accepts her man totally but in our view something in her isn't quite right either. Feel into why it isn't, Martin. What do dream lovers not have that Annie has, for example?"

"An edge. It makes the dream lover feel a little bit wishy-washy."

"Absolutely. Annie's loving has edge, doesn't it? What does edge give Martin, for example?"

"A sense of being 'in there', of caring enough to participate."

"We feel the 'caring enough to participate' is very important, isn't it? Why important?"

"The dream lover is a doormat. She could almost say yes to anything."

"A doormat isn't very motivational really, is she? Why isn't she motivational?"

"With any being who constantly totally accepts, I might become lethargic; anything will do, all is acceptable."

"Absolutely. So on balance, which would you prefer right now?"

"You know the answer, because the dream lover would become boring after a while."

"Absolutely. So do drop the dream lover. Of course all men have a dream lover. And, as we have seen, so do women. We feel Martin is now able to tune into a woman's dream lover. He has uprightness in his bearing. He has a very high self-regard. He is able to remain warrior-like without worrying about the other man's immortal soul. May we suggest Martin tells us the sense he has of a warrior who does not worry about the other man's eternal soul."

"There's a sense of ruthlessness about it."

"Absolutely. Feel into why a woman is drawn to the warrior who is ruthless, right now."

"He's on a horse with a lance. The maiden before him is prostrate and offers herself to him, in the sacrifice of giving. The woman wants to be 'taken' by the man. She has no control over the man who is so rampant, so ruthless that she suspends everything and gives her body to him.

"It is exciting to have no control over the dream lover, to throw caution to the winds, to set yourself aside and let him take you. It is exciting to be controlled by a rampant and powerful male. But it's not very practical because when he's had you he'll move on and have someone else."

"Women feel loved and let down so often. We feel the most valuable part of the dream lover syndrome is that it keeps the principle of marriage and family alive in the psyche. But the new era is coming when the dream lover will change in principle.

"Martin, what is happening with your new dream lover now, in her white frock and more rounded figure?"

"There is more discussion between the two partners, not a melting of the woman before the man. A meeting of minds as well as a meeting of bodies. There's equal passion in all things."

"But we feel a change in the essence of the dream lover?"

"It becomes more tangible, less dreamy, a more <u>achievable</u> dream, rather than a dreamy dream, a waking dream. It isn't fantastic, but possible."

"A daydream, perhaps. Tell us the difference between a dream and a daydream."

"A daydream is a rearrangement of realities. A dream is fantastic, it's fantasy."

"We feel Martin can also see the 'ideal man' changing."

"He still has hairy legs but the armour goes. He is now pervious, but still exciting. The prospect of the approach of the dream lover still makes for great excitement, but now of a confirming relationship not ravishment and abandonment."

"What is the most fundamental difference, though?"

"His understanding of the woman and the caring for her eternal soul."

"It is a different way of protecting the woman, isn't it? How different?"

"The protection is absolute."

"How does the woman react to that level of protection?"

"As she feels the continuing strength of his protection, she is able to remove her shell and become skinless."

"How does that make her respond to the male now?"

"They feel totally together; passionate, sexually. Wow!"

"But she does surrender in some new way, doesn't she?"

"It is a surrender, but not a thoughtless surrender."

"We feel the way forward now will be to look at how a new dreaming of the lover allows a new dreaming in the way of the world. We feel Martin is able to tell us what the couple who are daydreaming are able to accomplish. What are their daydreams, now?"

"The immediate response to their closeness is a peace of extraordinary depth. They live in harmony and through this, wish also to live in harmony with their surroundings. Anything else would jar their wonderful relationship. So they look to the wider world for ways of replicating their own joy and harmony and making the world safe and peaceful."

E for Empathy

The way to resonate with the partner is to empathise. This is a way of experiencing the other's position in any given situation. Someone who can empathise with another human being is able to resonate to a frequency that mirrors the other person's experience. It is a way of resonance that allows one person to empathise with another person's feelings.

Empathy is a gift, and it is a gift that many people already have. But when someone comes up against another's negativity, in a way that makes them feel extremely angry or anxious, empathy stops. A brick wall comes up. If someone is making you feel angry or anxious, then empathy flies out of the window.

We feel to have real empathy with someone who is in emotional pain, there needs to be a level of detachment. Empathy is possible even with someone in the family, but probably not if they are on our doorstep. If that person's pain is right inside our home, then it is not always easy to find ourselves in sympathy, let alone empathy, with what is happening for them.

Partners often make each other the butt of their own feelings of inadequacy, fear, rage or pain, and we suggest there needs to be a method of detaching from a partner's pain, which allows us to remain in empathy with each other. It is impossible to feel empathetic towards someone who, when they are in pain, is constantly reminding us of our own failures. It is not easy to remain detached if one partner is making the other the scapegoat and always sees themselves as victim.

It is the victim mentality that needs to be released here, because no one is a victim to someone else. We are only victims to ourselves and our own negative patterns. A real management of victim consciousness is important if relationship is ever to feel like a real partnership, and not just a battleground of insecurity against insecurity.

We feel the way to remain detached in such a situation is to make sure you put a barrier up in front of you against the barrage of blame from the person who is scapegoating you. Feel the barrier like an impermeable plastic sheeting in front of you. Then really listen to what the other person is saying, knowing it cannot permeate the plastic sheeting.

Allow the person to speak their feelings, if you can. It is not easy to listen to a catalogue of disaster without feeling drawn into the victim's will, but a level of detachment can make the other person feel heard. Hearing the other person is the most important thing in any partnership; hearing how the partner feels, and allowing that feeling to register with a deep hearing inside, without quickly making a judgement about what they are saying.

Everyone on the planet is hurt. Everyone reacts out of these hurts in partnership, but it is very important in this era of huge shifts and changes to make sure the victim feels heard, and that the hearing comes from a detached place. There is a responsibility now, on all human beings, to witness the victim inside themselves and recognise that they are their own worst enemy. No one is victim to anyone else's 'margin of error', by which we mean that no one is victim to the way someone else is feeling pain.

We feel there needs to be an understanding of how the 'margin of error' works inside people. If we feel emotional pain, we have a place of pain inside us that no one can assuage until we have found the reason within ourselves for this pain. It creates a margin of error within and round us and we always feel pain when this margin of error is hit. We always react to this pain in some way, often by hitting out at others, and there is nothing anyone can do about it – except us – until we can release that pain.

Until the pain is recognised, understood and released, other people will hit your margin of error and it will feel as though they are hurting you. The way to recognise the feelings that make you recoil in pain (your own margin of error) is that someone – usually the partner – hits the spot again and again and again.

Empathy, then, for the person whose pain spot you keep hitting, is a recognition of their margin of error, and the trick is to learn how to stop hitting it. There is, in empathy, a way of recognising someone's pain threshold and not hitting the spot. It is recognising how to help make that pain place more manageable and allowing the person to feel safe in that place of pain, until the place of pain is recognised and released.

Empathy, then, is a way of creating, for others, a safe space to look into their pain places inside, and really allow them to feel safe enough to explore and manage the pain. It is a means of helping others to allow the pain to be heard and seen and released safely.

May we suggest that this is a task for the new millennium because until people are able to hear what others need to say, particularly those very close to them, there cannot be a shift towards the new partnership of equality, empathy and enterprise.

*   *   *

"We feel Martin is able to become registered into a frequency that is able to take into account Annie's feelings. He can remain himself, yet do a check into how Annie feels about a situation. This is a technique which is available to others to help them know how another feels and empathise with them. We feel Martin is able to take a leap of faith, in the sense that he is not totally convinced there is an easy way to feel other people's feelings.

"We feel Martin is able to become open in the solar plexus now. Feel what needs to happen inside, to become open in the solar plexus. Give a detailed account of how that happens."

"You go within your head for a moment and then slowly slide your consciousness down the inside of your body, like a fireman descending a pole. Slide down to your solar plexus and be aware of a gaping hole there which looks outwards onto anything you wish to make connections with, to probe or feel."

"We feel Martin is able to locate the solar plexus for us, by feeling what extent it covers."

"The solar plexus is slightly above the navel. It reaches up to the rib cage and spreads across the entire width of the body. Activating the solar plexus regularly, it can become even larger. It's quite surprising in its expanse, it is a very flexible organ."

"May we ask Martin to tell us how he was able to locate it the first time."

"With difficulty. It felt like a cave and it was dark. With regular use the tunnel opens up. It lets in megawatts of light and makes the arena quite vast. It's a wonderful stage that appears to get larger and larger as you use it. Initially you are looking for a pinprick of light."

"Why does the solar plexus enable you to witness other people's emotional states?"

"The solar plexus is the central seat of emotion in the body. From it radiates all emotional channels, receptors. It is the nerve centre, the bus station for emotions."

"It is the switchboard, isn't it? We feel Martin will tell Annie what she is feeling now by this method. Tell us what you do to feel the feelings."

"I go inside myself to the solar plexus. I stand on the stage of the solar plexus. I say I'd like to find out how Annie is feeling and it just happens. It is like a resonance set up between us; an energy link, and somehow I seem able to feel an overview of her state of being, how she feels."

"And what is Annie feeling?"

"Jumbly at the moment, a million thoughts: houses, watering plants, the garden, a telephone call, mother, writing."

"How does Martin receive this information?"

"Mostly by fragments of pictures, sometimes by sounds, a voice, or perhaps just a feeling inside."

"Absolutely. Now we need Martin to make this technique safe for the person he is enquiring about. What does this technique require in order for it to be unthreatening to that person?"

"You must enquire only with the well-being of the other in mind. That's the first rule. You don't enquire for power or control or anger, merely to find out about their well-being."

"What happens if someone asks in power?"

"Blankness, a brick wall. The solar plexus is blocked like a rockfall. You are denied access. It is only to be used in love, or the solar plexus is 'removed'."

"The safety valve is there automatically, isn't it? But more than that, what happens to the enquirer's well-being if he usurps the privilege of helping the other?"

"It feels as if he takes on the other's angst."

"We feel the use of power backfires on to the enquirer who will feel dreadful. So we feel Martin is feeling Annie's feelings now. May we ask Martin how he can empathise with them rather than be upset by them. Empathy means recognising and relating to the situation."

"One way is to bring a little of that energy down the connection and place it – their understanding – in the solar plexus; siphon off a tiny bit and place it within you. The second way, you just tune your vibration to theirs."

"Annie, you do it automatically. But, yes, Martin, we feel either explanation is valid because when the person's vibration is mingled a little, the enquirer is able to empathise. Now Martin, still feeling

Annie's feelings, is something able to 'help' Annie to remain cool under her many feelings, as it were?"

"I feel it's fine to send a calming ray, a feeling of calmness along the connection, providing it's not controlling, merely offered on a human level as a kindness by one who empathises."

"Absolutely. To offer it is to leave the acceptance to the person concerned, isn't it? Not to impose how that is received on the unconscious level."

"It is received on the unconscious level almost as if a gate is opened to allow it in. It is examined on the unconscious level and if it is accepted that it comes in peace and love, the guardian opens the gate and receives the vibration. If the vibration is unacceptable – if it is controlling or angry or unpleasant – it is sent back, marked 'return to sender'. By the law of the Soul it is bound to rebound."

"Be reassured that we speak of what many people do naturally, but many others find impossible to do. We feel Martin is able to tell us what Annie did with Martin's calming ray."

"I feel it radiated round her body."

"And what has that done for the relationship?"

"It brought us closer; made us closer on a vibrational level."

"Absolutely. But more than that. Can the relationship move into another realm of experience?"

"The picture I get is of a pipeline between us which expands with increased usage. The link is a very powerful one and will become an alternative conduit for the spoken word."

"When empathy is in place, speech becomes less important, doesn't it? So the misunderstandings of speech are lessened, aren't they? Empathy allows communication on a very deep level. Empathy is a deeply spiritual way of relating. Why spiritual?"

"It is the form of communication used in other dimensions. They don't talk to each other, they send and receive feelings."

"Men are a long way behind in feelings, aren't they? But if they can feel empathy with their partners, their lives will expand beyond their wildest dreams."

F for Fire of Intention

The element of fire needs to be realigned in some way to allow water to be experienced differently on the planet. Water needs a new relationship to the incredible element of fire. Fire was the element that brought the mountains into being. Volcanic activity started when fire at the bottom of the planet began to move and have its being. This made the water element somehow less able to express itself in the way it had done when water was the only element on the surface of the planet. Now water wishes to recognise itself in a very different manner to the way it has done over the series of millennia since volcanic activity began on planet Earth.

There is a new matter happening in the planet. As the Earth warms up through the rage of those people who are carrying Earth's rage, there is, if you like, new volcanic activity happening on the planet. This is making the water element feel even more exposed in some way. In our view it is a natural phenomenon that water should begin to fight back, and indeed in some places water is truly terrifying people by rising up and making itself felt. The coasts of many countries are threatened because the water element wants to realign itself within the human psyche and within the planetary being.

Water is unable to become the element that makes Earth peaceful until fire is held in check. What needs to happen is a recognition of the destructive nature of fire and how fire needs to be subdued now in the human psyche. The human psyche, of course, carries all that is within it and all that ever shall be, even though so very few people recognise that fact. The Earth itself, and every human being, carries within itself all that is within the Universe, in one way or another.

Water, then, makes up most of the planet and most of each human being. Yet the fire element is making it difficult for water, not only to hold its own, but to realign into something even more relevant to a new humanity in the next millennium.

It goes without saying that relationship plays its part in the realigning of Earth to water in a new way and releasing the need to be so fiery. There is now an opportunity – as Pluto, which is a mirror image of Earth at this time, makes its journey through the fiery sign of Sagittarius – to recognise the deep truth that fire within the human being is now destroying the planet. We suggest that those who are able to let go this fiery Earth dynamic will start to relate to the Earth and to others in a more watery manner; in a more dynamic, detached, flowing manner and not in the fiery, emotional way that many people would agree they operate out of now.

"May we suggest that Martin takes himself into a place of watery flow – and not the place he so often inhabits, the fiery magma inside the Earth. What is the difference in feeling, Martin, in the watery flow, to the fiery magma? Because Martin also does know the watery flow place very well."

"The water has a lightness of touch, it's much more gentle and flowing ....."

"And detached?"

"The fiery magma seems to draw you in, suck you down – it's like a mud hole, a muddy swamp that devours you."

"Absolutely. Devouring Mother, isn't it, this black hole, this swampy, raging, fiery magma place? It is a devouring feeling and Martin recognises this fiery feeling of being devoured by the magma – yes? It's a place of no return like the magma place that burns you up – maybe a bit Hieronymus Bosch even. This is hell on Earth, a place of being devoured by the fire in Earth. And that is how the hell place has been described.

"But if they're honest many people are already in hell sometimes; in this being drawn towards the fiery depths of Earth, unable to be in the more flowing place that Martin experiences sometimes inside. In fact, Martin can stay in this watery flow now, can't he? Why is that, Martin? What is to be gained by not being in the fiery swamp, but staying in the watery flow that is his birthright; his place of action now? And, why does he understand this flow now? What is the pay-off of having been in the magma for so long?"

"It feels like the magma is a descent into madness. Going in and out of it, one flips in and out of madness. The rage is an absolute madness."

"Absolutely. It's the place of madness that Martin knows very well at a very deep level, his descent into the magma. Indeed, all beings need to experience it in one way or another; not necessarily in the mad way, not in the sexual way, but whatever is the deepest fear of each individual needs to be found and released.

"The most difficult thing for the woman too is to release the fire element, because she is only just beginning to realise how fiery she is capable of being.

"We feel the most important thing we can offer here is the remarkable story of the moon. The moon was able to become the Mother of the Earth because, when the moon beings landed on Earth, they gave to the Earth beings a capacity to feel sexually. In fact, we feel a most important part of our work is to offer a more realistic light on sexuality.

"We feel Martin is able to become aware of the most singularly spectacular moonbeam entering his sacral area, right now. We feel it will feel marvellous to make room for the moonbeam. Is this possible? We feel Martin is able to tell us what happens when the moonbeam enters the sacral."

"It feels as though everything gets stirred up. There is confusion. All values, perceptions of sexuality, all are up for grabs."

"We feel you are not able to feel sexuality in the old way anymore when a moonbeam releases into the sacral. So we feel Martin can tell us how the old moonbeams brought sexuality in its current form to human beings."

"It feels like a compulsion, like an urge that has to be satisfied."

"We do agree that a level of fire from the moon brought an emotional charge with sexuality, didn't it? Tell us how this came about."

"It struck men and women in different ways. The female fire feels romantic but more passionate around romance."

"It is a passion in terms of relationship to a man, not to sexuality per se, isn't it? What does it mean to the male fire?"

"Compulsion. It makes it difficult for the male fire; the compulsion is like a fire on the veldt. It burns intensely and quickly moves on to possess and burn out and move on to another adjacent clump of grass, and so on."

"Absolutely. We feel moon fire came down to feed men and woman in different ways. Moon beings were androgyne but found there were men and women on Earth. So the androgyne split into two fires. What was the purpose of two fires on Earth?"

"It feels like programmed, karmic incompatibility."

"A programmed incompatibility. Now Martin, we need you to give us a more acceptable description because most people will find moon beings too difficult to accept."

(Martin sings) "Under the light of the silvery moon.... *Falling in love. Romance. It explains so much why the moon is held in such romantic regard."*

"It truly is. But tell us another way of talking about programmed incompatibility. What happens in women, technically almost?"

"Programmed incompatibility: a woman receives a man and begins to focus on him, solely, singly. Her gaze does not extend to other men. Her programme is to focus on her man with all her being in every facet. It is a wondrous focus; it's a very loving focus but there is a down side, in that it can become totally possessive.

"The male programme is constantly to view the horizon for interesting prospects, for exciting opportunities, for beautiful bodies, alluring offers. Men are attracted to the scent of women. Not truly programmed for monogamy."

"Absolutely. We need Martin to tell us how the moon was responsible for this state of affairs. May we suggest it is to do with power, that the fire was brought by those moon beings who were into power. Tell us how power comes into it."

"There is a sense of power both ways, in both programmes. Women want to possess in such a way that it becomes a power issue, rather than acceptance. And men want to dominate, to ravish as many women as they can. The power is in-built in both situations."

"Feel into the sacral region again and tell us what the woman's sacral feels about the moon beings who became power hungry."

"There is vast fear in the sacral. I see a large chastity belt around her."

"Feel the way the woman was programmed to feel most fearful of her free spirit."

"I have the feeling she is tied to a man."

"Absolutely The way women were made to stay monogamous,

while men did not, made the woman very fearful. We feel the distinction between men and women in this way was deeply fearful to women. Why Martin?"

"It made women feel like second-class citizens."

"Women were made to feel second-class citizens by the moon, not the true moon beings, but by renegade moon beings who were into power.

"We feel Martin is able now to feel into the new moon. The new moon will feel very different. We feel the old moon beings brought fire away from the moon and left her cold. We feel the new moon is now warming up because women have been hitting back at their programming.

"May we suggest that the confusion in relationships is happening now because the moon is sending down moon beings again. Sexuality is changing once again. Feel in the sacral what is happening to women's sexuality; to women's new fire energy."

"It is still focused on a single relationship – women aren't eager to be promiscuous. But when they choose their partner, the feelings are of relationship without power. Not the obsessive bind."

"How about passion now? What does that look like?"

"Very nice. Loving, but different. A feeling of surrender. It means not controlling, but welcoming your lover with an acceptance of all he is and isn't."

"We feel the acceptance of imperfection is vital. We feel that before then woman needed perfection. Why?"

"Because he was the chosen man. She idealised him. The programme stated that he was a God and by definition had to be

perfect. The realisation that this man wasn't a God, just a man, was bound to lead to disillusion at some point. So every relationship was on a downward trajectory."

"Return to the new moon again. Feel into the sacral and tell us what the new fire makes Martin feel about male sexuality now."

"It smells different. There's an odour of purity about it. It does not need to seek out conquests because there is a feeling of satisfaction within a one-to-one relationship. There is no programmed dissatisfaction."

"We feel a new 'fire of intention' is carried, instead of a 'fire of power', isn't it? What does that mean?"

"The fire of intention means that people are able to visualise a future for themselves and this future is achievable. There is no more rosy glow which by definition causes disappointment."

"What does that mean in terms of relationship to sexuality?"

"It feels like <u>making love</u> rather than, for her, powerful possessiveness, and for him, ritual rape."

"So what part will the moon play now in the sexual relationship between men and women?"

"There feels a lightness of touch, rather than the heavy hand of compulsion like before. A gentleness brought about by the beings of the moon."

"We feel the moon is able to let go in some way now."

"The karma of the old programmed relationship bound the old moon to Earth and to Earthly relationship. With new relationship coming into being, the moon is released."

"The child releases the mother, doesn't it? Now, feel the difference in fire for a women, allowing her to let go a kind of resistance to her own beautiful sacral area."

"It feels more relaxed in the sacral. I sense she is now on a lighter burning sexuality, not an enormous smouldering heavy-duty bonfire. A gentle perfumed fire."

"A spiritual fire, isn't it, Martin? A fire of surrender. Tell us about humanity's spiritual fire."

"It is more gentle. In theory it doesn't seem very different."

"But in terms of surrender by the woman, how does this match in the man's experience?"

"A sense that the woman's surrender takes us down a notch of understanding and closeness, which enables the man, through her surrender, to come down a notch, which allows the woman to come down a notch. It's a programmed deepening process which surrender initiates."

G for God

We feel the way forward now, is to understand the meaning of the 'God within'. Until the God within is understood there can be no real understanding of interdependent relationship.

"May we ask Martin what he feels in terms of God now, as the judging God in the sky? Is He a real God or a father figure to the planet in some way? The man in the sky who says 'Thou shalt not' mostly, and who is unable to realise that men and women want to make a bid for independence from 'Thou shalt not', to become their own masters in the sense of realising their own way to morality and integrity.

"What does this Father in Heaven feel like, Martin?"

"It feels very stagey, a fixed perception of God, a very necessary perception of God. But almost a projection into the sky of the needs of the community."

There was the need in the early Christian times for a Father-God who was able to protect His people as a father once protected his children. The Father-God is a decision-maker. Within the psyche of the people, over whom He moves and has His being, the Father-God is the 'authority over'. The Father-God is the one who makes His children behave properly, come what may. And, in our view, this is the cause of so much fighting in the world, because there is one God who knows best for His people.

We sense the Father-God was a projection of maleness onto the Father-God, because there was also the need to worship. The authority figure <u>was</u> worshipped. But, now, all authority figures are crumbling. All the male-dominated ways of doing things are manifestly not working any more, and authority figures are no longer in authority in the way they were.

Women in particular, have decided that the father figure male is no longer appropriate for them. They feel the father figure male has not served women in any way whatsoever. They see him either as patriarchal – in that he is the one who knows how it 'should' be – or manifestly as the warrior male who was the dream, but whom it is no longer possible to marry.

We feel there needs to be a leap of faith that the Father-God has been usurped in terms of what women can accept as their male authority. We feel women are becoming their own authority and cannot allow men to dominate them any longer. We feel the way forward then is to reperceive this father figure God in a new way.

"May we suggest that Martin is able now to feel himself in a market place of great dimensions. It is like a Greek town in the Middle Ages, perhaps. A real cut and thrust market place because Greece, more than any other culture, was a cut and thrust political culture and men were the market leaders, so to speak.

"We feel Martin is able now to recognise himself in this cut and thrust market place manner, really enjoying this male-dominated culture. Can Martin sense this market place culture where trading happens, with men the leaders of political and financial matters?"

"Intrigue. It's an intriguing place to be, but there's definitely intrigue going on."

"Absolutely. We sense that intrigue was rife, wasn't it? May we ask Martin what the feeling was then, at that time, in terms of what power did for men of worth, as it were? Corruption is the outcome of absolute power, isn't it Martin? In what way does power corrupt? In what way is power a corruption of life itself?"

"It feels as though the level of energy in the market place was very

high, it's very frenetic and there seems to be a high energy to power ... it's very fast. It feels as though there's a sexual component to it as well. There's an excitement, a frisson about power."

"And corruption? What happens in the framework of power that corrupts, Martin?"

"Is there an element of jealousy about it, or ... I don't quite understand the connection ..."

"Absolutely. Jealousy."

"It's as if ... if you could have a purity of power – as an example, an early Chinese emperor – then that might be possible, but immediately you put power into society, suddenly it's surrounded by people who don't have power, who have things they want to trade with power or who want to be associated with power. It's a very dangerous thing – power. Seductive."

"So this culture of male power is seductive, yes? It makes people feel high energy? And money becomes the God, doesn't it? The high energy of the male power syndrome is money, not God, yes? How does money become God, and not God, Martin?"

"Money is the means by which power is traded, it passes hands. I suppose God is only an energy, money is a more physical manifestation of the power."

"Absolutely. So power, corruption, sexuality and money become God, don't they? And God Himself is no longer worshipped in the same way, is He? Why not? What is God's problem, if you like?"

"God is the wrong dream. The dream becomes avarice, possession, power over."

"Absolutely. And God, Father-God, who was worshipped, isn't the same as the worship of power any more, is He? We feel, therefore, that it was the changing nature of power that was responsible for God's demise, at some level, and that this has been purposefully created in order for the God within to manifest, to become more appropriate.

"May we suggest that in the scheme of things God the Father cannot be the God of mankind now. The way forward will be to recognise the authority figure within each human being now and not to project authority onto other people.

"We feel Martin is able to understand his own relationship to authority, perhaps. We feel Martin is able now to feel a tingle in his left arm. We want to locate this tingle in the funny bone and to suggest that it feels odd to have a tingle in the funny bone, yes? What's this feeling, Martin, this tingle in the funny bone?"

"It has to be humorous."

"Of course. We feel Martin can tell us, in the funny bone, why he finds authority so difficult now."

"Well I suppose, off the top of my head, it just feels totally inappropriate."

"Why? What is inappropriate about feeling other people have total authority over you, as indeed you always felt they did? Yes? Can Martin feel why that's silly?"

"Well, I suppose the answer's two-fold. One is that they didn't, it's what I imagined that they had. And two, once you've moved away from that position, you can only be responsible for yourself."

"Absolutely. We sense the way Martin saw authority figures before was as a father figure of judgement, yes? He projected God, if you like, onto almost everyone he met, men and women alike, and this caused him huge difficulty, didn't it Martin? May we suggest Martin takes a view now on why he saw everyone as the judge, somehow – the God of judgement out there making a judgement on him."

"Is it to do with power?"

"Absolutely. May we suggest the idea of power was very exciting to Martin then and, of course, he corrupted power in some way, because absolute power corrupts. So, in terms of this need to feel powerful he turned it in on himself to feel totally powerless.

"We want people to understand that people see what they need to see in terms of external processes. The people of Christ's time needed God to be all powerful and wise and a judge, because they were not ready to retain their own inner relationship to authority.

"So, Martin, we suggest the work we have done together has released the aspect of 'power over', which resides collectively in the male psyche. We suggest to Martin that he finds it amusing now to think that everyone on the planet has authority over him, yes? How does it feel that the world no longer has power over you – that you are in charge of your own life now?"

"It's shocking, There's disbelief that I could ever have thought the reverse and there is a great sense of freedom and, inevitably, the responsibility for my own to-ings and fro-ings from now on."

"Absolutely. The most valuable way of recognising God within now, is to recognise the commitment to that recognition and to making the promise of feeling totally responsible now for the way life is. When the Father-God is brought within the human being there is a knowing of Godness within. The way to recognise God within is to recognise a sense of one's divinity, which is a process along the path to becoming more human now.

"We feel this level of self-responsibility will be really important in the coming years, as life becomes more and more difficult in some ways. And if the God within is firmly held, then no one can unseat the way of the individual – as opposed to the way of power over – in times of difficulty.

"May we ask Martin, however, to be aware that when a man is able to recognise his God within, the woman who understands her God within is in a really safe place. Why? Power over has gone in its real sense and the powerful nature of this relationship is really there, isn't it? What is the way of two people who feel totally self-responsible, independently of any external authority, but who choose to come together now?"

"The feeling is of a balance. It's a see-saw certainly, they go up and down, but it's essentially a balance."

"Absolutely. May we suggest Martin needs to really make sure the God within feels married to Annie. How does that feel Martin? What is the difference to marriage now?"

"It does feel different in that in the past I've invested Annie with power over me and the transition is quite mega, in coming to a place of the God within for me, so that we are on the level playing field we all talk about."

"We feel that old habits die hard and within the relationship the projection of being powered over will make Martin feel insecure, until the way is found to manifest this God within in a really deep way.

"May we ask Martin what this makes him feel, suddenly, because he is able to release the power marriage now?"

"It makes me feel that I've got internal work to do or to work for myself on myself. I know the things that I want to do, which I think will put that in place."

"Absolutely. The way to see what God within feels like, is to recognise that the separation is important, before the interdependence is put in place. We sense men and women of courage will be able to separate out from old patterning and move into a new relationship of independent interdependence."

H for Humour

May we suggest that humour is the cosmic joke. There is humour in cosmic reality because humour is the energy of cosmic manifestation. The cosmos is not real. The cosmos is, in fact, illusion. It is a figment of God's imagination and therefore it does not exist . We do not exist. You do not exist. We are all an illusion of a great illusionist.

It isn't easy to be human, is it? But, in the word human is the word humour and the word humus. It's all compost, isn't it? May we suggest that there isn't any truth, any reality and indeed no illusionist, either. It's all illusion, isn't it?

Life, like Einstein said, is relative and everyone is relative to everyone else. It's the way it is and ever shall be. Relativity is relationship and relationship is about relatives. It's all of a piece and it's all about separation and it's all very funny, isn't it?

That's how the cosmic joke works. It is all so seriously conducted in whatever way people conduct their lives – economically, practically, creatively and relatively. It's all relative. It's all illusion and it's all in the cosmic joke. So, whatever you feel about life, remember, there's no reality at all to it, and yet it has to be taken very seriously indeed, doesn't it?

*　　　*　　　*

"May we ask Martin to sense into that humorousness of the existence of cosmic realities, now. Can he sense how it needs to be acceptable to mankind? It's about recognising how life creates itself. How we create ourselves and create the universal relationship to mankind. It's all illusion, isn't it, Martin? How does that feel suddenly?"

"I'm thinking about Annie saying the other day that people were

standing upside-down on the other side of the world and wondering how it could all happen at one time. How does the Universe retain its integrity when such ridiculousness takes place and everyone thinks they're standing upright? You almost need to have a serious vein to keep you going, otherwise you would just stop and say 'It's all too ridiculous, what are we doing here? Let's all ... well, let's all sit around and laugh, it's too silly."

"May we suggest Martin feels into the seriousness of how it all is and makes a start at looking why 'meaning' needs to be uppermost in people's lives now, and not the never-ending race, principally to get more money."

"Well, there's a sense that all else has failed. They have given consumerism their best shot and that doesn't seem to work. But it's more fundamental even than that, there's a change of heart within people."

"Absolutely. There's a changing heart, isn't there, and that's why meaning has to be recognised. So recognising meaning in life makes it more humorous, doesn't it? Why Martin?"

"The more you look into meaning the less meaning there is in some paradoxical way, and that has to be funny."

"May we suggest humour is a meaningful means of finding meaning and in our view, humour needs to be recognised in the serious search for meaning. We feel so many people who take life seriously don't recognise the fundamental underlying relationship to humour, which is the cosmos. It's all humorous. It's all humus. It's all about being human.

"So, Martin, feel a real energetic input in such a way that it concerns humour but is very, very serious indeed."

"Somewhere or other a sunflower is emitting a ray, a sun ray.

There's a particular ray which emits a humour of deep understanding. Not cynical, not putting down, but humour with lightness of touch. It enables people to cope with the vicissitudes of life together: the loo overflowing, the physical ridiculousness of making love, the non-availability of good coffee! All things can be seen within this ray, which enables whole generations of people to get by stylishly. High humour, loving its accepting nature. It acknowledges the twists and turns of life as experienced in this dimension."

"Tell us where the sunflower is rooted in a human being."

"In the genital region for men. In the navel for women."

"Two yellow sunflowers; from the penis and the navel. That's humorous enough in itself, isn't it? So feel the humour of the humorous sunflower. Tell us how it feels itself making the human being humorous in the unfolding times."

"It reminds me of Ken Dodd's tickling stick, the sunflower."

"What does it mean for new relationship to prosper?"

"There's a lightness of touch; a humour about the penal sunflower that needs to work its way into relationship. A sexuality of lightness of touch. The concept of perfect sex needs to be consigned to the bin. The seriousness needs to go out of making love."

"But it needs to apply to life in general, too, doesn't it?"

"H for humour all around the planet. A way of viewing things."

"So what does the humour do, in terms of men and women not really understanding each other?"

"Men stop hating women and women stop hating men because they

don't understand each other. We treat it whimsically, this lack of acceptance of the opposite gender."

"It's a game now in some way, isn't it? What is possible when life feels humorous in terms of relationship to the opposite sex?"

"With that form of relationship there's a very touching bonding, a closeness, a trust, togetherness, unity, enjoyment at being together. At the moment, there's a black fug over the whole of humanity. Everybody needs to lighten up."

"The black fug is ridiculous now, isn't it? Why? What's happened already to make it silly to be so black about life?"

"There is a sense of opportunity around, an excitement."

"What opportunities can become available if the world lightens up?"

"The opportunity to be so creative in every sphere."

"Now feel the T'ang Dynasty of China. We feel the humour of the Chinese. Tell us why humour creates creativity."

"Almost everything created in the T'ang Dynasty came from humour. Humour was the way it was talked up."

"Now feel the Chinese humour. We feel Martin can look into his sacral area and feel how sexuality felt in T'ang Dynasty China."

"Comfortable."

"We feel humour can make comfortable sexuality. Why?"

"It's a ridiculous thing to do."

"So feel the Emperor and Empress in the role of Master and

Mistress of a thousand concubines. Remembering humour creates creativity, there was, we suggest, a revelation in the T'ang era that to release semen through concubines created more humour in the nation as a whole.

"If Martin takes this imagery back into relationship he can tell us why the release of semen will create humour, and thus more daily creative living."

"A concentration of sexuality into humour rather than domination or performance, then the participants take on a rosy glow."

"Feel into that possibility. Does it feel good?"

"There's a stained glass window – a figure with halo; a very early Christian image."

"Absolutely. It is Christ-like to create humour, isn't it? So feel what a partnership of daily light-hearted creativity will bring to others in the environment."

"I see it as something to be tapped into."

"Absolutely. No more deep and meaningful in the old way, is it? Tell us what that means for women now?"

"Doing things in a style of living. It is no longer about a box that contains a repository of information. It is not about a deep knowing, but allowing everything to flow. All energies to mingle and come loose. The tide needs to ebb and flow for every opportunity to be creative in its own particular way, with lightness of touch. The word is exquisite."

"So sum up H for Humour, Martin."

"Life was always so serious. Now there is a move to a very

different, creative style of living where we see ourselves and our loved ones and all around us through a delightful cloud of non-abusive humour, which gives a light touch to our lives, especially the most serious events in any relationship.

"Making love was viewed almost as a service, like a Church service, a ritual that has since lost its meaning. By reinvigorating our love-making with humour we can experience a new dimension."

I for Impact

We feel the most important way to regard relationships is in the impact they have on the outside world. It is not just the two people concerned who have a relationship together, they also have a relationship in the outside world which has an impact on other people. There is not just one energy facing the world, but two energies dynamically intertwined. If the relationship has a 'margin of error' between it and the outside world, then the outside world will not benefit at all from the relationship, nor will the relationship benefit from the outside world.

There needs to be a recognition that 'Dyadic Partnership', now, is a way of working for the collective good in the world. It is not just two people coming together to create a relationship for themselves. The dyadic partnership will actually be a force for healing on the planet. When two whole people are able to come together, in the sense of both being healed and clear of their negative patterns – of their 'margins of error' – then the dyadic relationship itself will create a vortex of energetic resonance around it that will be a force for healing in the world. It is not difficult to see that two people who are harmonised energetically inside themselves, will have a different impact on the outside world.

In the coming years a real effort can be made to release the patterns that keep each individual in a 'margin of error' state. In our view, it has been women who have taken the lead in releasing themselves from this 'margin of error' resonance in the world. It is women who have recognised themselves in a very new way over the last thirty years. They have, if you like, released a lot of negative patterning, simply by coming out in the manner of the woman of substance.

What has been happening over these years of the feminist cause is a bringing out of the masculine nature, the 'animus' in Jungian terms, which has allowed women to express themselves consciously in the world; doing so has allowed a new level of consciousness to emerge in the world.

However, in the process many women have manifested this masculine aspect to an excessive degree, to the detriment of the full integration of the masculine and feminine parts of themselves. They have remained stuck in a maleness that has created new difficulties for two people trying to relate together as man and woman. In recent years it has often seemed more like man and man. This has been confusing for men, particularly those who have lagged behind in recognising their own unconscious female aspect, the 'anima'.

In our view, it is now up to men to begin to find a relationship to their inner feminine but, more than that, to move on into a new and fuller relationship to a truer masculine. And the vanguard of women who have moved through the animus phase to a new and deeper relationship to womanhood, will be the mediators of this new maleness.

May we suggest that there are many women, now, who have been able to work with their new male analytic consciousness, not to be a surrogate man in the world through their heightened consciousness, but to further plumb the depths of feminine awareness. They have touched a new and profound level of womanhood that will soon be recognisable in the world. It is they who will initiate men into a different kind of male leadership.

And so there is a huge sacrifice to be made now on the part of women. To let go, yet again, their hard-won male skills, in order to allow another, truer feminine to arise. This new woman might even look quite similar to the original feminine kind of woman it was so hard to escape from. A shocking prospect, isn't it, that the woman who spent so long finding her own deepest knowing about herself will have to release that recognition yet again, in order for the impact of dyadic partnership to become a force for change?

*   *   *

"We feel Martin is able now to experience the impact of a dyadic partnership. We feel Martin can sense himself in a room which is not lit up very well. He feels himself in a darkened room, in a place that feels a bit oppressive. It is not easy to get your bearings in this room, is it, Martin? And there's a sense that there is someone else in the room, but it's almost too difficult to see. How does it feel?"

"It makes me feel sick."

"Why sick? What's the problem here? What is the darkness feeling like?"

"It's almost as if I'm looking for myself and I can't find myself."

"Absolutely. There's something wrong inside, isn't there, that seems to regard the being in the room as part of yourself that you can't get at, yes? What's the feeling like?"

"Well, it feels like a shadowy figure that is almost just a blackness that doesn't have any shape. It's just like a black shroud."

"May we suggest there is something in the room that would help Martin to feel less uneasy. What is in the room now? It's a woman in white, we suggest, who could help you in some way. What's the feeling that this woman engenders in you somehow?"

"Firstly, a calmness, it's a reduction in fear."

"Go on. What else does it feel like?"

"It feels as though I can move towards this woman – the 'woman in white' – and through her get to the black shroud. She's a way forward."

"Go on. Why is she a way forward? What's the difference in energy between this woman and the black shroudy figure somehow?"

"The black shroudy figure feels like death. It feels so frightening, so fearful, that it is impossible to approach."

"Absolutely. And in some way this 'woman in white' is able to recognise the fear you are feeling in a way that is quite extraordinary. Yes? Tell us about this recognition of the fear somehow. What is her skill in recognising the fear you have about this shrouded figure?"

"Well it seems that intuitively she understands it; she experiences it. There is a sense almost that maybe it's no big thing, it's sort of practical."

"Absolutely. Knowing this woman understands the fear, there's a difference in the feeling, when you saw a shrouded figure in black? What's the essence of a seeming fear that changes its nature because the woman is in a position to know the fear?"

"Well, it feels as though the fear is illusory. It exists, but I think it must be within me. It's just understanding the fear within me."

"Absolutely. And in her wisdom, the woman knows this, at some level, doesn't she? So she can reassure Martin that there's something to be faced but it won't kill you off. Can Martin really feel the sense that death is averted by allowing this woman to hold the level of fear, in some way, because she knows that the fear is illusory? What's the sense you get about the deal here?"

"There's a sense of a trade-off almost. You put yourself in the woman's hands to come through this experience safely. You can't do it alone because the fear is so frightening it feels as though your Soul will be removed. So you go through a mediator who holds you and allows you to approach it in a way that is less frightening, or perhaps even not frightening."

"Why is she able to hold this fear for you? What was her task, then, before you met the 'woman in white'? What did she manage to achieve that had to be achieved before she could help the man face his fear, his deepest fear, of death, at some level?"

"I think she had to go through the process. I could feel the sickness of her fear in facing the same situation."

"May we suggest the woman took the decision to descend into death at an earlier stage, didn't she? To pave the way. Why did she choose to do that – to face her death fear before returning to help the male do so without death happening?"

"I don't think men were ready to enter that particular room and there's also a sense that because women almost have responsibility for birth, they seem also to have taken responsibility for death."

"Absolutely. In the past women held responsibility for life and death, didn't they? It is in the system. As women give birth so they understand death at a very deep level, or have done so far. It has been the woman's task to allow birth and recognise death inside their deepest being.

"Women who have decided to tread the path of consciousness have taken either the role of birth or the role of death. It is not easy to be a mother, but women trod the path of birth – gave birth to babies who were their children.

"Other women, many of whom did not have children, decided to tread the path of death on behalf of mankind. It's easy to recognise that now, isn't it, Martin? We suggest Martin has benefited from the experience of Annie's treading the path of death, yes? That is our way of describing the journey for Martin over the last years. He faced his greatest terrors, which in some way were held by Annie, and now, we suggest, he is able to become a man of substance in a very different way.

"If Martin can make the leap of faith that he has encompassed the shrouded figure now and is standing beside Annie in a different way. Tell us how this feels in some way that now creates a completely new impact outside. What is the difference between a 'woman in white' with a man still chasing his fears, and a 'woman in white' with a man who has conquered his fear of death?"

"I think there's a completeness about the second situation. There is a wholeness about the relationship and it feels as though external things that happen to the second couple can be faced, just faced and dealt with; whereas in the other – the 'woman in white' and the man beginning the journey, everything is internalised, taken personally, and then brought into the relationship, which makes life very, very difficult. The other situation is one of completeness, of feeling integrated."

"And how is that integration played out energetically into the world outside? What happens to the resonance, if you like, of that new relationship?"

"Well, I do see a light. It does feel very beacon-like. It feels as though others might see it as some sort of answer."

J for Jarring

May we suggest that where a woman is not able to release the 'warrior woman', there is a jarring in the system. We feel jarring is what happens, now, because men cannot take anymore of the warrior woman. There is a real tension in the relationship between the warrior woman and the man who somehow knows he needs to descend into the shadow of his being, because the warrior woman is unable to help him.

The 'woman in white' we speak of is no longer the warrior woman. We feel it is only the 'woman in white' who has integrated her masculine animus persona into a new level of the feminine, who can offer the man the space he needs to descend into his own deepest fears and anxieties. The warrior woman threatens this man deeply and, in many cases, the warrior woman has no feminine resources.

Some women have become so male that their testosterone levels have risen. Or they are faced with operations to correct difficulties in their feminine hearts, so to speak – ovary cysts, hysterectomies, are symbolic of the way women have been unable to recognise the deepest level of their feminine being and the feminine parts are making themselves felt.

Some women, too, are over-male in their attitude towards men. They cannot stand men in some ways and are competing with them in all respects, now. This jarring in relationships causes confusion. Women need now to take responsibility for looking deeply at how over-masculine they might be, mentally and physically, too, sometimes.

Many men, of course, are beginning to recognise their feminine qualities. The New Man is evident in the man who wishes to look after children and be part of the feminine territory. And yet, we suggest, there is still more for the man to discover. Unless women release their hold on the mental activity which men traditionally have been the guardians, they won't really understand the new feminine way of being in the world. And the men will be precluded from becoming 'real men' with all that entails – as opposed to feminised men, which has perhaps been an interim experience.

For men, now, there is an urgency to descend into the Earth realms and to understand their relationship to the Earth in a practical way; in some ways in an even more practical way than women. And in our view, it is up to women to recognise that their part in the relationship between men and women is changing profoundly. There is an equalising of relationship, but not in the way that most men and women might imagine. It is an equalising by finding out who each person truly is individually as man and woman, and then recognising the profound difference.

*   *   *

"We feel Martin can experience the jarring that happens when two people are in relationship 'in the wrong bodies', so to speak, in the way that many men and women are experiencing now. Even the body itself is confused.

"So, Martin, we feel there is a situation in which a woman is the warrior woman. She has a great job and she is up there in the forefront of business acumen. She is very attractive: She is stunningly 'on the ball'; a woman to be envied by other women. And that is the problem, we suggest. There is an enviable quality about such obvious success in the world because for so long women have been trying hard to be equal in the workplace.

"But, put the boss next to this warrior woman. What is his feeling about this woman who is such a whiz-kid – because, although he is the boss, he feels rather confused about his role now, doesn't he? What is his feeling in the face of this wonder woman who can raise children and who can be up there alongside the best of men? Is he happy with it?"

"I think it's a mixture of resentment, fear and perhaps confusion. I think he doesn't know what to do, or how to approach."

"Absolutely. There's no approach mechanism is there in the situation? Whereas if Martin sees the office typist, say, there's still a method of approach. It's rather sexist, this approach, isn't it, Martin? What's the feeling here about a typist who's looking very pert and pretty, right now?"

"Well I think there's a physical attraction towards her from the boss."

"Absolutely. It's more about 'ogling', isn't it Martin, that makes the boss feel something else, yes? Not like the wonder woman makes him feel. So, there are two situations here that are both unappealing really. Can Martin tell us how it feels for the man in the street to have these two messages going on inside?"

"Well, I will speak for the man in the street, because it is terribly confusing. Being human and male, you peg people – you meet somebody who you think is one thing and you find they are not what you first thought. When that happens it's really confusing.

"For example, a disabled colleague had a care worker with him when we went out for lunch together. Suddenly you find out that although she's working her way around the world, she's really a hot-shot lawyer from Australia. You suddenly realise this gorgeous girl is rather brilliant, and you're thinking 'Oh, what did I say?' It's really quite funny, but it's not."

"Absolutely. So what is the conclusion here about how the man in the street feels about women in general right now?"

"Well, to be honest, I think you back off and you treat each encounter with a danger sign. I think that's the way society is constructed at the moment, you close off, because it's not safe."

"Absolutely. It's not safe is it? Relationship is fraught with danger – it's jarring, isn't it? Can Martin feel that jarring between men and women now? Describe jarring, then, Martin."

"It feels like a shock, a reverberation through the body, through the heart almost."

"Absolutely. So, what happens to the man in the street's body mechanism, if you like? What happens to his heart for a start?"

"I think it gets enclosed, it looks to me as though the man in the street locks himself in a capsule."

"And in his genital region what happens? There is also a real jarring there, isn't there? What happens?"

"I think it all freezes."

"In the sexual regions."

"It's almost as if it goes away."

"And the sperm count reduces. Can Martin feel that? In his confusion the masculine rejects confrontation and the sperm don't want to come out. Is this possible, Martin?"

"There's a feeling of... I think the body feels that they're not received and therefore it doesn't produce."

"Absolutely. There is a sense that the woman doesn't receive anything anymore, and sperm want to be received, with love and blessing, don't they? Can Martin sense this feeling that women no longer receive men? They approach men, they attack men, they love men and they hate men, and the sperm can't bear it. Can Martin sense this almost collective sperm withdrawal in the situation? There is a real feeling in sperm consciousness that they can't go places anymore in love and comfort.

"But we suggest that the attitudes of both women and men need to be taken into account. Men have been very aggressive in their attitude to women. Men have always wanted to become the power over women, and in the last years women have been rebelling against that. It is this that has enabled women to become men within themselves and to take over the male roles mentally.

"Indeed, we suggest that when they are able to connect to it, women have more mental agility than men, and that creates tension. Women can undermine men very easily because they have a very clever way with their agility of mind.

"So women don't respect men anymore and they can't receive men anymore, because they have no respect for them. In many ways, women are smarter than men, aren't they? What does that make the woman feel? When the man is confused and the woman doesn't respect the man?"

"I think they look down on them."

"Absolutely. The authority figure is no longer appropriate, is it? Women no longer need men to be in 'authority over', do they? No man is an 'authority over' anymore, and the women aren't able to respect men anymore. The jarring is complete."

K for Knees

The knees are such a significant part of the body. We want to speak about the importance of knees, right now. Knees are the place of humility. We feel knees are the place where we decide whether or not to recognise humility within. A real test of whether someone who is offering help to others has humility, is to ask them to kneel down.

"Kneeling down is not easy, is it, Martin? What is the feeling inside when you kneel? Is it uncomfortable in the back, for example?"

"Yes."

"How uncomfortable?"

"It puts tension in the back."

"Absolutely. It puts tension in the back. Now feel into the way it feels in the heart area when you kneel."

"It feels very closed off from the heart's beat."

"Absolutely. Now stand up and feel in the heart what it's like to stand up. What is the feeling now?"

"It feels suddenly open."

"Absolutely. Now can Martin kneel down again and tell us what the feeling is in the heart now. A resentment, we suggest. There's a resentment about making you kneel again in quick succession."

"Yes, I suppose that the puppet comes into play, a feeling of being controlled."

"Absolutely. Now feel it deeply, this feeling of being controlled because we have asked you to kneel in front of the people you are hoping to help by doing this book."

"I feel deeply embarrassed."

"Why embarrassed? What is the feeling?"

"I think that it's humiliation. I feel a little humiliated. I feel there's a large congregation ....."

"Go on. What is the feeling of having to kneel in front of this congregation, then?"

"I'm being singled out. It feels almost ritualised humiliation."

"Go on. In what way is it ritualised humiliation to be on your knees in front of the crowd now?"

"I feel it would be fine if we were facing the same direction and we were all kneeling together, but somehow I feel very confronted by this."

"Go on. What is the deepest feeling about being on your knees now, in humility? What's the sense about how these people see you?"

"Could it be as an object of scorn or ridicule?"

"What is that feeling about, Martin, the feeling of being scorned because you offer humility by being on your knees?"

"Could it be a sense of inadequacy?"

"Absolutely. There is such a deep sense of inadequacy in people that they cannot bear to offer themselves with humility. May we suggest this is the way many people feel about this most difficult aspect – of being able to offer what they have to offer with a sense of humility.

"It is not humiliating to be humble. There is no humiliation in just being who you are, humbly, and without any need to stand up in an exaggerated way? There is such a need, now, for people to be really humble inside, which is not about being 'ever so 'umble' in the Uriah Heep sense. It is about each individual recognising their true worth as a human being.

"There is nothing wrong with feeling worthy. It is a most valuable way of making sure the life is lived fully and completely. But so many people are feeling unworthy, right now, because they fear their lives are not up to scratch in other people's eyes. Life, though, is no longer about looking good from the outside. It's about looking inside and finding the goodness within, and thus being able to recognise how difficult it has been to feel your own humility. Only when people have delved deeply into their patterns of unworthiness and can feel a measure of their own self-worth, are they able to operate in humility.

"May we ask Martin what he feels now as he stands up to face the crowd? He feels himself extremely agitated, we suggest, in the sense that he cannot feel himself fully in the situation. He is feeling inadequate to the task, isn't he, and he feels very unworthy to stand up in front of these people he wishes to help. Why, Martin? What is the feeling?"

"Is it a fear? Is it a fearfulness?"

"May we suggest there is a deep fear inside and Martin almost cannot stand up straight, can he, because he's so unworthy in his own sense of being. So he puffs himself up and he feels taller and grander, and in that puffing up he becomes what? Too inflated, yes?"

"Over reaching."

"Absolutely. He feels far too inflated, suddenly, inside. Yes? What is the feeling now in front of these people?"

"It feels like a lot of hot air coming out."

"Absolutely. It's a lot of hot air, isn't it? That feels more comfortable, but it isn't valuable the way Martin feels it should be. So he feels even more inadequate and so he puffs himself up even more to feel adequate and then he feels sick and tired and miserable, doesn't he?

"Make the decision to stand next to the 'woman in white' again and tell us how it feels in the situation, because she is feeling secure with him there. And yet she can feel a humility about herself, can't she, this 'woman in white' next to him? What happens to the man, Martin?"

"I think the pressure is off."

"Absolutely. Why is the pressure off? What is the energetic feeling next to the 'woman in white', who knows she is adequate to the task and yet feels humble inside?"

"I feel it is perfectly possible to look people in the eyes, to stand without fidgeting, to feel comfortable and to say it how it is."

"Absolutely. There's no need to fear, no need to puff up and feel even more inadequate, is there? Now, go down on your knees now Martin, in the situation, and tell us how it feels to be humble, in the face of people you are trying to help."

"It feels like service, no more and no less."

"Absolutely. Service in the face of a need, isn't it? No humiliation, not puffed up. Just feeling it just is."

L for Landscape

We feel that landscape now needs reperceiving. It is not what it used to be, the landscape of relationship. Because the way things are right now, the landscape of relationship has become blurred, and in our view, there needs to be a repositioning of the landscape.

There needs to be a real understanding of how men perceive women and how women perceive men, and how the landscape lies in the relationship between men and women. There is a need to distinguish between the way men perceive the landscape and the way women perceive the landscape, in order for life to move forward. The men and women who are to relate in a new landscape, need to become aware that, indeed, the landscape has changed.

We recognise that men and women have been battling rather over the last years and, in our view, there needs to be some way of recognising that the landscape of the one is indeed extremely different to that of the other. We feel Martin and Hannah can see each other's landscape perceptions, if you like, and even how their landscape perceptions might change – if they are happy to do this for us.

(Hannah is a friend who was visiting at this point)

"We feel Hannah is able now to recognise the landscape she inhabits. There is a whole vista out there in front of her, and it's so vast she can hardly manage to recognise that there is a landscape at all. It is so vast it sort of melts into the distance and she cannot even recognise herself to exist in this landscape. Is this possible, Hannah? Tell us how that feels – to feel the landscape is so vast that she cannot even recognise it as a landscape, somehow."

H: "I'm actually having a sense of myself just as a tiny dot in it now, but from that dot, as I look around, it's as if the images go past me so quickly that it's very difficult to say what it is I'm perceiving. As

I move, or perhaps I'm spinning, so quickly in the centre of it, the images that go by are very blurred, because there's so much there."

"Martin, what is the feeling in this vast landscape that passes by so fast Hannah can't even see it happening, somehow?"

M: "In this landscape I can only relate to a very small area, I think, and it's very static, not much movement. It's like a flickering image in a cinema, it's too fast, flashing lights in a disco, it bewilders."

"May we suggest that even though Hannah is bewildered by her own landscape, Martin is feeling unworthy because his landscape is so small by comparison. Tell us what Martin's landscape feels like suddenly. In the extreme of Hannah's whirling landscape, his landscape is like a pinprick by comparison. What's the feeling, Martin, about your landscape now?"

M: "It's parochial and very minute, as if it's the small picture, it's the nitty-gritty. It seems as though I'm focusing on just a tiny little patch."

"So in some ways you feel inadequate, but also your patch is totally clear. While Hannah's is vast and not clear at all. What does Martin's landscape feel like, Hannah? In its clarity and its smallness, if you like?"

H: "A wonderful refuge, a place of calm and rest and peace and a place from which to be able to look out onto this huge landscape, without being lost in it. A place of stillness from which this vastness can be viewed without getting totally lost in it."

"Absolutely. It's making Hannah feel a little unworthy, isn't it? Like Martin felt unworthy, though his patch was clear. Hannah feels unworthy because her patch is so big. And yet, in between, there's some space for both men and women to stand now. Can Hannah feel herself walking out of that small space now into her landscape. What's the feeling, if she knows her small space is there and safe, or perhaps that Martin's small space is there for her to step back into if she feels too lost again?"

H: "It just feels like a wonderful relief; it's something I really want to be associated with."

"May we ask Martin how to find a bigger landscape for himself, then, in this double-take landscape situation. What's the answer to reperceiving the landscape itself, perhaps, Martin?"

M: "I'm actually having quite a lot of difficulty walking out of the small patch; it feels quite prison-like. Walking through the garden gate's quite difficult into the bigger landscape, into the hills. Or I'm seeing Hannah's as a sort of Australia – very large and I'm really quite afraid of it ...."

"Martin is afraid of the larger landscape, isn't he, and Hannah is feeling rather ambivalent now about her landscape ideal. What's the situation now, Hannah? Because Martin's landscape might feel very safe, but it's not easy to get out of, once you're in it, is it?"

H: "No. There is the real feeling of wanting to be able to share both views, to be able to somehow bridge the fear or the lostness, to be able to share both views in order to be able to encompass the vastness, but without any hindrance of a fear or a holding back, somehow. I don't know if that is making sense."

"Absolutely. So, that's the point. Men have such a small landscape and women have such a vast landscape inherently within them. There is a totally different landscape inside men and women, and Martin and Hannah both recognise the collective situation in their extreme landscape pictures. It's the difference between men and women and Martin and Hannah represent the extreme of that experience. Now, what's the solution, we wonder?

"Martin, find a solution. What is the way a man can perceive a woman's landscape as unthreatening? Hannah what's the way a woman can perceive a man's landscape as not imprisoning? What's the way forward, Martin, to recognising how to enlarge enough to start encompassing a woman's landscape view?"

M: "I think in the past I've used my small plot as a place of safety. When I'm out, I retreat to it in my mind, I pop back there. So I can go out and I go back in, to myself – into the garden. It's almost as if I've got a piece of string which pulls me back into the garden so I can find my way back if I get lost. I know I can find my way back."

"Absolutely. But what can Hannah tell Martin about how to expand now into the vastness at a new level, perhaps? May we ask Hannah from her experience of the vastness, how Martin can begin to change his landscape perception, perhaps."

H: "I'm not sure if I'm answering the question directly, but my sense is that I want to really trust and value the fact that there is that base and that place of safety, and to really acknowledge the fact that it's there as a sort of microcosm/macrocosm thing, actually. That the vastness is all encapsulated in that small space, so that in really trusting that is there, the trust can be taken out into the much bigger space."

"Can Martin sense the ideal that, in fact, within is the all, and that man can have it all from the sacred space, if you like. May we now ask Martin to tell Hannah how she can stay in her void and experience the little plot landscape in order to feel safe still."

M: "I think it's very clever because it is the same argument almost in reverse, isn't it? Every giant space is made up of microcosms so presumably wherever you are, you will be quite safe in your own little space."

"Absolutely. Find the mechanism to allow Hannah to feel herself in a bubble of safety in her macrocosm experience, Martin. What does she need, to find the small space in her own being, to stay in the everything space? What's her need then?"

M: "Is it to go within the heart and find it there?"

"Absolutely. May we ask Martin what he knows about the heart as a protective bubble place in the macrocosm?"

M: "It's very encompassing; it's terribly protective; it's very safe."

"May we ask Hannah. Martin's vision is sound. Why is it sound, Hannah, in this regard?"

H: "I don't know, I find it difficult to quite get a sense of ...... I suppose the heart is actually that space. Yes, that is the space. Again ...... it's the space within the being human – it's the link between the vastness of the all and the vulnerability of being human."

"Absolutely. May we ask Hannah to <u>sound</u> her place of safety."

(Hannah uses sound as a therapeutic tool with clients. She makes the sound)

"May we ask Hannah what her feeling is now in the vastness place now."

H: "I feel much more where I am, that the vastness is there but it isn't breaking me up."

"May we make the suggestion that Hannah sounds for Martin his ability to make his landscape bigger now, from his small point of reference."

(Hannah sounds again)

"May we suggest Martin makes his feelings known from that sound base."

M: "I thought the guides were going to ask me to sound it myself. If I had I think it would have been very close to that tone – maybe a little higher."

"Would Martin like to sound his place?"

M: "Yes. (he sounds) *It immediately made me think of the possibility of raking leaves in the garden and being somewhere else at the same time. Almost another dimension, but certainly a different place and not wrapped up in prison."*

"Absolutely. Now, Martin, describe the in-between place that men and women can meet now and describe how that landscape feels. What's the difference now?"

M: "Well, it looks like a pasture which is level – a more level playing field I suppose you could say, on which to inter-relate."

"And Hannah? Is that a feeling you can endorse, somehow, that there's a mid-way point of contact?"

H: "Yes. I have an image almost of ... well, first of all, it was hands linked with a big space in between, so that it's an open-armed sort of embrace, but at arm's length holding hands. And then the image became one of crossing hands – so that it became a figure of eight link so that there is a link, but there are two spaces. Somehow, being able to move between that one big space, between the two, and the link with two separate spaces."

"May we ask Hannah to tell us if her issue has somehow been resolved now. In a way that makes her recognise something that is now possible?"

H: "Yes. It's having the two, the movement between that one space and then the separate spaces and yet there is still the link. And that seems to be a symbol of a personal relationship, as it were. But also the relationship between the macrocosm/microcosm. Moving out into the vastness of the all, and yet having the connection with something that's close enough to be able to be encompassed and feel safe."

"Absolutely. In our view the landscape is changing and it is changing for the macrocosm and for the microcosm, inside each human being. It is represented by men and women who are seeking to understand their own nature. Indeed, the nature of men and women is changing and the landscape in which they move and have their being is changing. Men and women are relating in a different landscape."

M for Marriage

"We feel a cold coming on, Martin. It is a rather runny-nosed cold, isn't it? What is the feeling like, somehow? Not very nice, is it, the feeling that Martin recognises inside himself, right now?"

"I think I feel all right inside myself but there the sense is that it's a constant dripping of the nose which I have to keep blowing."

"This is a feeling Martin has, in the most remarkable way, now that he recognises it. It's like a constant need to blow the nose. Of course Martin doesn't have this constant need to blow his nose, but there's a feeling that things just go on and on and on in some way. There is a leakage always in some way. What is the feeling that we are contacting for you here?"

"Is it like a battery running down? It feels like a loss of energy. Is it allied to me feeling tired?"

"Absolutely. There's a leakage of energy, isn't there, all the time, that Martin doesn't really register often, but it's in there, isn't it, Martin? And today you feel that way, yes?"

"Very much so."

"There's a leakage in the system now, isn't there? What is that feeling, Martin, because Annie has it, too, all the time. She knows she's leaking energy all the time. What is a more plausible explanation of the leakage right now? May we ask Martin what the feeling is about this leakage, of the tap dripping all the time, in some way?"

"I'm aware of my feet being on the Earth. I'm also aware of me not being on the Earth, of being almost in a bubble in space, that's safe

and there's no energy. But it seems like a problem being encountered on Earth where energy appears to leak away."

"Absolutely. May we suggest it is rather like Annie's coffee pot, it's getting up steam, but some of it is leaking out of the sides before it gets to the top part, isn't it? Can Martin recognise that for him, too, there's a leakage in the middle rather than at the top or the bottom? There's a leakage out of the instrument because the two ends aren't quite locked in together, like the coffee pot isn't quite sealed? What is the feeling, Martin, in the middle? There's a leaking out because the seal isn't quite solid between the top and the bottom. The energy can't quite come up into your being and leaks out into the etheric fields?"

"Is it connected to the emotions, because it feels as though one bleeds there?"

"Absolutely. It's the solar plexus chakra, that registers all the emotional material. In fact, we always ask clients to feel their psychology in the solar plexus because that's where the emotions register most profoundly. And, of course, it's the chakra that also analyses the feelings. Mind-emotional energy is there in the solar plexus, so it is a good place to register all the difficult material that is making a person unable to complete their life in some way.

"So there is a leakage in the system that is being healed, bit by bit. We feel Martin can tell us why Annie, too, still feels she is leaking badly now, even though she has actually tightened up the screw, as it were. What is the situation if someone else is drawing on the emotional body all the time?"

"Is it osmosis?"

"Absolutely. It is pulling out the leakage in someone else. So, in fact, this is a way of describing how one person leaches energy from another when they are leaking energetically themselves because the emotions are still very raw. The other partner, however balanced in their own emotional state, will be pulled out of alignment. They will leak even more than the one who is off-centre. Does that make sense? The clearer partner will be more energetically drained, because the energy is being drawn out into the other partner's etheric field."

"This makes me feel very sick."

"Why sick?"

"It does feel like a bottomless pit."

"May we ask Martin what that feeling is like; that this leakage is never going to end because the emotions won't stabilise."

"It feels pretty desperate."

"Absolutely, because there's such a terrible wastage of energy."

What needs to happen is an integration of spirit and matter in each individual so that the Earth's energies can rise up without being waylaid by the emotional body in the solar plexus where they leak out. It truly is the most rewarding life if the Earth can contact the spiritual body of the human being without the emotional body disturbing that energy flow. It brings about the possibility of the marriage, within the human being, of Heaven and Earth.

The pit isn't bottomless. There is no sense that the emotional body will never be healed. It is in the evolutionary process now that mankind can and will release his emotional body, the astral level of experience. Karmic material will be cleared once and for all, so that Heaven and Earth can join together within the individual and on the planet now.

So what is the issue right now, deep down, that provokes this 'I won't let this bottomless pit go, even though I know and have experienced that it is possible to let it go'? We feel strongly that a stopper needs to be put into this bottomless pit, a halt made.

Because, yes, mankind can keep going down the bottomless pit towards the terrifying places of madness and fear and raging Earth, but may we suggest it is time to cap that bottomless pit. Mankind must no longer be allowed to 'go down' too far. Indeed, surprising as it may seem considering the yearning for the spiritual search, nor does man need to go so high into cosmic realities that he loses touch with his humanity.

There is, if you like, a realigning within the human being of the human material level and the human cosmic level. The marriage of Heaven and Earth is on Earth, not in the realms of cosmic Godliness and certainly not in the realms of material terror that were inhabited in days gone by when the animal level of humanity was in place.

It is time to release the deepest, terrifying animal instinctual level of humanity in order to 'move up a notch'; and re-balance cosmic realms and material realms within the human being, in a way that is appropriate for humanity now.

May we suggest that if a human being gets caught into the material bottomless pit of Earth's instinctual matter, he is lost, as the Hieronymus Bosch vision shows. Conversely, if he gets stuck in the cosmic realms – as people can do, for instance, if they have taken drugs – it is possible to stay out in realms where human beings are not meant to be. There now needs to be a damming up of the material bottomless pit, and a stopper put onto the cosmic realities that many people believe they are seeking.

Each individual is being asked to acknowledge his deepest unconscious negative patterns, but there is a danger too, in delving too far, for too long. As James Hillman suggests, the Titans are not in the human domain and do not need to be encountered by human beings. Nor do the spiritual realms of cosmic miasma.

It is hubris to imagine humanity needs to delve into the darkest places. And hubris to believe that it should be telescoping into the deepest realms of space. Man must stop delving and soaring, and stay human now. That is all that is being asked of him: to stay human and create a marriage of Heaven and Earth on Earth, through the Soul of mankind. Humanity always wants to go further and further and further. But it is more important now to stay inside the human experience, where all that is, is.

May we suggest that no one else is involved in this; no aliens from outer space, no Titans from the underworld. This is about the human being making an attempt to become fully human now, and in that attempt to remain human. The marriage of Heaven and Earth will happen on Earth.

Marriage itself is about staying within the human framework. Marriage is about making men and women love and respect each other above everything else. Above the need to discover space or dissect the atom at its deepest material level. That is about hubris, and man is becoming a hubristic being now. What is needed is a recognition of what it is to be truly human, and what it means to marry Heaven and Earth within humanity.

N for Nothing

"We must ask Martin to feel into nothing now. It is not much, is it, nothing? We feel nothing is a space inside the being, isn't it? What does the nothing feel like Martin? It's nothing much, is it?"

"It feels like a sort of silvery pinprick, a silvery pin-head."

"Absolutely, that is nothing, indeed, isn't it? A silvery pinprick. May we ask Martin to describe nothing, in some way that makes him feel suddenly rather interested in nothing?"

"It feels as though it's surrounded by a great deal of space. It seems like quite a journey to get there."

"What, to the nothing?"

"Mmm."

"Absolutely. What is the feeling about the nothing place that makes Martin find it interesting?"

"Well, I have a sense that to get to the nothing place you have to sort of take off your back-pack, all your baggage."

"Why is that so, Martin? What is the feeling that you need to get rid of all your baggage, luggage even?"

"I suppose it's the human condition. If you arrive with something, it isn't nothing."

"Absolutely. We feel there is a real recognition, Martin, that you have to arrive at nothing with nothing – practically bare, yes? That's the conundrum. You can't find nothing if you're covered with luggage and everything, can you? There is such a paradox here, because there is the journey to nothing, but you can't get there if you're stuffed full of patterning and habits and things. What does that feel like, if you start off with so much luggage? You can't even begin to contemplate nothing, can you?"

"I suggest you can walk past nothing and walk over nothing because you're so busy exhibiting your patterns and remaining true to type. You can't sense nothing at all. You can't see it, you can't feel it."

"So nothing isn't there really, is it, if you're in the habit patterns of lifetimes and lifetimes? So, Martin, look at nothing again and suddenly drop everything you're feeling in some way. What's the feeling?"

"The feeling is that I instantly go to nothing. It's like playing 'Monopoly' and landing on 'go to jail'. You get a 'go to jail' card and you just arrive."

"Absolutely. If you let go everything that has been hindering you, you land up at nothing straight away, don't you? It suddenly isn't a huge journey. There is no space between you and nothing if you start letting everything go, yes?"

"Yes."

"It's a relative nothingness, isn't it? There is a relative space and then no space at all, if you start off at nothing, suddenly."

May we suggest there is relevance here in really allowing yourself to make a plan to let go everything you are now. There is a sense in the Universe that man is changing beyond recognition and that if he holds on to his baggage, there won't be a recognition of that incredible shift in mankind's being. There will be people who don't even know that there is a nothing place and won't even recognise that other people are in this place.

There will be a dimensional shift in the energetic framework of planet Earth and some people won't even recognise it. But others will, and there will be, if you like, a two-tier system on planet Earth that is very odd indeed. Some people will be going about their business, in a way that they recognise, while others will be going about their business in such nothingness and joy and pleasure at being a different human being, that the two layers won't even know they are in a different framework.

That is rather a difficult concept, isn't it? But in our view, what is happening now is a journey to nothing and in that nothing place there will be a meeting of Heaven and Earth, and in that meeting of Heaven and Earth there will be a different planet Earth, even though many people won't even know it has happened.

"May we ask Martin what feeling he has in the nothing place, of letting go the luggage, the baggage of the karmic material he has carried for aeons and aeons of time."

"Surprised that I haven't done it before."

"Absolutely and it is so easy, isn't it? Just to let go the baggage and find the nothing place, suddenly. Now, feel yourself in this place and describe how humanity will be on planet Earth, in this new human being place."

"I don't know if it's possible to describe. It feels like a clarity there, but it's so wrapped up in the immediacy of 'now', it depends what people decide to do, doesn't it really? It appears there is no future so I can't say. I mean, I suppose the only view you can have of it is from outside. And because I can say with some certainty that there is going to be a Labour government tomorrow and the Queen will still be Queen and I'm going into town, that all those things will be the same but, in some way, nothing doesn't predict anything. I don't know."

The way humanity has lived, so far, has been in a sense of time that has a past, a present and a future. The reason for this is that the emotional body in touch with moon rhythms has had to be present in order for mankind to evolve through the karmic 'cause and effect' patterning. In some ways, this has kept mankind the slave to cosmic forces because there has been a pattern maker, if you like, who has made patterns. It's almost as if God were a pattern maker and mankind had to keep to the pattern.

Of course, mankind has evolved from the most instinctual being to a conscious being and that has needed time in space, because there was the rhythmical, cyclical nature of moon-time to evolve humanity. Now, however, humanity is moving towards the moment at which time is no longer needed in space for those who have reached this point of release in their karmic history.

May we suggest that time will no longer be experienced in the same way by those who have let go their karmic history. 'Now' is all there is, and now is the point at which every human being takes total responsibility for their now moment, and therefore for their future experience.

It is scary, isn't it? And Mother Moon has held everyone in her embrace to feel safe, as mothers do. But, as in life, mother is being let go at a profound level within each human being and within the Earth and, in fact, by the cosmos. And now mother isn't the guardian of everyone's circuitry, as it were.

The moon has been responsible for the circuitry in mankind – the water element in mankind – that has kept everyone in a circular historical patterning, but now the moon is leaving. In fact, scientists, too, recognise that the physical moon is moving in relation to the Earth. Man is no longer commanded to stay in a patterning of cosmic making, but can join cosmic mankind in the now moment. Man will be the arbiter, not only of his own destiny now but, in many ways, the arbiter of cosmic motion too. It's a daunting prospect. It is also incredibly exciting that man is coming of age now and the child in the cosmos is becoming the adult, who has responsibilities to cosmic evolution.

We feel the way forward for partnership, then, can only be

recognised when 'nothing' is recognised because the partners in the situation, who are also at the now moment in space time, are different.

"May we suggest Martin is able to tell us why partnership cannot be as it was in moon space time."

"It feels as though in moon space time we were dancing to a gavotte – a patterning. We had the ability to make it into the twist or the lambada, but we still danced to the dance – we danced to the music of time. But now, I think that's not appropriate. I think we're released from – being released from – this tied relationship, which tied into the human relationship, a sort of triangular, circular thing which we couldn't get away from."

"And partnership isn't tied, is it, by watery, elemental moonbeam energy any more? What is this like, Martin, the tying of the watery element to moonbeam energy?"

"It feels as though we were always at sea, we were always in a silvery river of emotion which on occasion was flooding and we were paddling hard. Sometimes we were swept downstream by it, sometimes it was quiescent.

"Always we were in this undulating stream of emotion which, for me, was certainly tidal and connected to the moon. There was always this emotional hold of the moon and I can see us getting out of the boat and walking onto dry land and sort of shaking it off. Almost, this is circular because it means that the emotional drip can now, with the turning of the tap, be switched off. Human beings can turn off their emotional tap and allow the energy to come up from the Earth, and be connected to Heaven."

"Absolutely. It is the decision, isn't it, to let go the Mother that can allow the emotional drip to be stayed somehow. Not needing the

Mother, whether in moon terms or cosmic terms or real mother terms or partner terms, yes? The Mother is making her exit now, at a very deep level, and the children of Earth are growing up independently now, aren't they?* Can Martin sense how partnership will feel now?"

"I'm seeing a teddy bear walking along on its own. I wonder if one of the implications of that is that in relationships, either one or both parties were teddy bears, just playing at it. It was a game somehow.

"It was like being in the kindergarten. There were certain rules and regulations and ... teddy bears could only be teddy bears, they can't be a lion or a tiger. You can only be a teddy bear, and you can only be what teddy bears can be. Teddy bears are teddy bears, but to release yourself from being a teddy bear is to allow yourself to be anything."

"Absolutely. Teddy bears have captured the imagination of the entire world, haven't they Martin? And Martin can see why now. What was the teddy bear able to confirm in the human being, at some level?"

"Teddy bears were always teddy bears. It was as though, in a sense they were always there and they provided warmth and cuddliness. There was a constancy about them – your teddy bear was always where you left it, and therefore you could always turn to it when you needed it. The paradox is that it could only be a teddy bear but it could provide you with the warmth and the love and affection, and always be there for you at a time when you were emotionally distraught as a child."

"And now? The teddy bear isn't quite relevant is it?"

"Presumably, that's why the Teletubbies are so big."

"Absolutely. The Teletubbies are absolutely 'now' creatures and, in some ways, they have been responsible for allowing the separation of mother and child at a very young age. It is no longer 'listening with mother'. It is very complex indeed, but no wonder the Teletubbies have hit big. It is in the psyche of letting go mother, and becoming independent information beings. Does that make sense? May we suggest that partnership will be so different and teddy bears will be swept aside now for Teletubbie people."

* This theme is explored in detail in Tess Nind's book 'The Everlasting Relationship: Mother and Child at war and peace'. Published by Rowan Communications Ltd.

O for Oppression

May we suggest something that is probably apocryphal. Women are more fascist than men if they become over-male. In the last thirty years, the feminist cause, which, of course, was absolutely necessary, has created in many women this over-the-top male. As we said earlier, it was necessary for the woman to recognise her inner male to allow her to become conscious of herself in a new way. But the feminist ideal has often created in women more maleness even than in men.

This could be surprising, perhaps, to many women who still feel they are unable to match men in their daily lives. But, in fact, the most important thing to recognise right now, is that a level of maleness is set inside women, which means that not only do they recognise consciously their male aspects, but also sometimes allow those male aspects to run turkey around men.

We suggest that women who have discovered their male 'animus' are indeed recognising themselves as women of substance. But, in some cases, the woman of substance has become a woman who knows too much. She is able to run rings around men mentally, and this creates the feeling in women that men are not as clever as they thought themselves to be – or, indeed, as women thought them to be. This has created a rather unpleasant conflict between men and women, particularly in situations where there are high-powered relationships.

We sense inside many women is a woman who knows best and it is the woman who knows best who can pull the rug on men very easily. They are able mentally to tug the rug from beneath men who recognise they are on a very slippery slope when confronted by a competent female mind. But this female mind may be fascist in attitude. In fact, the fascist aspect of maleness is more prevalent in the woman who has over-done her male side, than in the man who has that measure of the feminine within him. This man is less mentally agile than the woman who believes 'I am the one who knows'.

Many men have discovered their inner feminine now, and in that sense have created a more manageable maleness in some ways. But, in the same way, if they too have become over-female, they become a caricature, almost, of the feminine inside themselves.

There has been a really important shift in men and women to recognise the other gender part of themselves. May we bring your attention to the yin and yang symbol, where the yang side of the symbol has a tiny yin section and the yin section has a tiny piece of the male, yang, section. But when this reality happens in the unfolding process within men and women, at first there is a tendency to exaggerate that small piece of the other gender.

*   *   *

"May we ask Martin to recognise inside himself an exaggeration of female emotionality, which the feminised man sometimes creates inside himself. It is a very watery emotionality, and it comes out in an excessive manner in the same way that a woman's maleness often comes out in a caricature of maleness.

"May we suggest Martin can make the assumption that his life is not exactly over-feminised to such an extreme, but many men do recognise themselves as over-emotional in their feminisation. We suggest Martin recognises within himself an exaggeration of watery emotionality, which in some ways he doesn't like at all. But we feel he is able to recognise it for what it is – the feminisation of himself which is very practical and very deeply within him.

"There needs to be the recognition of how, in that exaggeration of the feminine within him, he is creating oppression – just as the woman who is over-male is creating a fascist oppressive relationship. May we ask Martin how oppressive this can be to a woman he is in partnership with."

"Does it tug the rug in the same way as the opposite does? Because I suppose in a way it upstages the womanliness of the woman."

"In what way? What is the effect on her womanliness?"

"I suppose that if you possess the emotional part of her nature for yourself, then the only area that she can own feels rather dry."

"Absolutely. We suggest that if the woman cannot be the one emotionally in charge, as it were, the woman's sexuality dries up in some way that creates a real sexual difficulty. The man feels rejected, and then can't understand why.

"May we ask Martin to feel what happens when a man's emotionality over-rides the woman's emotions in some way. Can Martin recognise this sense of making the woman's emotionality disappear, it's so quiet at some level? But if she is over-ridden by the man emotionally then she screeches her own emotionality at him in a way that creates even more difficulties. Is this making sense, Martin, to recognise that emotional oppression creates dryness sexually and screeching woman emotionally?

"Can Martin register this right now and tell us how it makes him feel? It is very important to recognise over-feminisation, as indeed we will return to the over-male situation, too."

"The first thing I want to say is how does the man stop it?"

"Let's look at the way he got into it, shall we? For many men at this period in history there was a dominant woman right from the start who forced him into being over-feminine. Many men fled into over-feminisation to compensate for a gruelling experience of the over-masculine mother. Does that make sense?"

"Mm."

"If men are to relate in a new male way, and women are to relate in a new female way, both need to stop the over-feminisation/over-masculinisation together. Both are oppressive, both are fascist in terms of oppression.

"What is the difference between the male fascist and the female fascist in men and women? What is the fascism of the man with the over-developed feminine?"

"It doesn't feel like a dictatorial oppression, which feels 'top down'. The over-feminised is 'bottom up', as it were. It feels as though there's a surge of water which puddles around everywhere and is very insidious and it's almost in the conspiracy theory area. It's sort of looking round and finding conspiracy lapping under the door. It's that sort of oppression, rather than the Mussolini/Hitler ..."

"May we suggest Martin now looks at the average woman's over-male abilities. See how they affect the over-feminised male. There is a tango here, isn't there, of the two fascists, as it were? What happens?"

"I think if the woman starts laying down the law he goes underground – he becomes devious and finds ways of doing what he wants to do without being caught, that sort of thing."

"May we ask Martin, then, how both can release the syndrome they are in? There is a real need for the woman, most of all, to let go being the one who knows, isn't there? It is the way life has always worked. The woman has led throughout evolutionary history and mediated to the man. And then the man leads from that mediation point. This is the point we want to put across: that in energetic terms, the woman is a mediator and the man is the leader.

"The more mature woman, the 'woman in white', who has descended deeply into her true feminine nature to recognise herself as a mediator, can now make that one further step and see that her femaleness is about receiving, not about 'telling it like it is'. She has achieved a wonderful level of consciousness now, but she needs to let it go again to reach an ever more profound level of wisdom.

"If the man is no longer the emotional extrovert, the woman can once again become a more emotional being. But not in the old emotionality; in a new, detached way that allows all that is to be experienced gently and potently, and more femininely, once and for all.

"What is the dual mechanism here, Martin?"

"It is the recognition, almost, that every notch that one goes up, the other goes up. So it's almost as if you climb the ladder together. That it's like a mutual reward, and so you see it, you do it, you see it, you feel it. And you get it back."

"There is a recognition of the 'itsy-bitsy spider' kind of 'up we go together', that will allow the man to let go the emotional oppressiveness now, because he will now recognise the difference between the fascist and the mediator in the woman.

"We feel Martin can now feel into how sexuality feels when the woman's emotional world isn't being dried up by the man's overblown emotionality."

"It feels very fluid, it feels very lubricated."

"And if the woman is mediator and not dictator, what is the feeling the man has about releasing the emotional extrovert?"

" It's like being given a good shove, to push off – to do it."

P for Premonition

We feel the way forward then is to realise that there is, in this moment of time, a maleness in women and a femaleness in men, and that this really needs to shift forward again. There needs to be a recognition in women – however they perceive themselves in the world – to make the sacrifice, if you like, of mental structural behaviour. There is in most women a need to be the one who knows, a sense of themselves as the one who knows best for themselves and for other people.

There is a way of using the analytical mind – the male part of themselves – by being the one who knows best. And in the male feminisation, then, there is a sense of relating to the partner as a woman of substance who cannot be crossed. There is a feeling that the woman changes the rules when she is in her 'one who knows best' mode, and it causes friction. Indeed, the 'woman in white' is in greater danger of doing this because she has learned so much about just how the world works.

Men, on the other hand, have to work with their feminisation in a new way, too. They now have to release the over-extended emotionality and recognise themselves again as men of substance in a new way. Men have had to become emotionally literate in order to descend into their deepest emotional relationship to life. But once that descent has cleared the negative unconscious patterning, and they recognise the desperateness of their plight, men need to realign to a different kind of maleness.

Of course there is danger here, of the male becoming over-male again and the woman over-female again. There is potential for difficulty and strife. But, there is also a way through, we suggest, which can help all relationships.

May we offer a vision of the future? But we also offer a premonition of what <u>could</u> happen, because there needs to be an understanding of the dangers, too, now. In some ways, there is even more opportunity for the fascist woman to arise and even more opportunity for the over-feminised man to erupt.

"May we ask Martin what the feeling is around the extremes of the male-woman and the female-man, now? How could this really make life very upsetting indeed, if the status quo were to continue as it has been for the last twenty or so years?"

"From the male side it feels as though the race will die out because of the lowering of the sperm count, and the emasculation of men would proceed apace."

"This is a real possibility, isn't it? Why is it such a possibility now? May we suggest there is more and more overcrowding and yet there is less and less relationship between men and women in a very real sense. What is the feeling about the cohesion of the planet, as men and women separate more and more in these extremes of opposite gender?"

"The polarisation is immense, isn't it?"

"Absolutely. There is a huge polarisation going on, not only between men and women, but in the atmosphere itself. And then the feeling is of what, Martin, in planetary terms? The dryness on the one hand and the over-wetness of the other is actually happening ecologically, isn't it? There is a terrible separation between fire and water at some level. What does this make you feel, in the planetary sense, perhaps?"

"It is almost as if the planet is separated. I don't quite understand it, but it looks as though the Earth could break into two and there's a sort of arid side; an arid piece and an emotional piece. Maybe it's a different dimension."

"Absolutely. May we suggest that in the scheme of things there is a danger that a separation between fire and water could happen and that deserts could become more desert and the watery, tidal situation could also become very extreme. This is an external expression of the separation of masculine and feminine in a terribly potent way. The over-extending of maleness in women and femaleness in men is wreaking havoc in the planetary sense.

"Now this may sound ridiculous, because how can the relationship between men and women create such a devastating effect on the planet? But, if you feel into the situation of current feminism, against the male's despair at the loss of leadership, planetary indicators move in accordance with this confusion, don't they?

"Feel how much the world has changed in the last thirty years as the difficulties have increased between the two representatives of planet Earth – men and women – the conscious beings on the planet, who have become so disparate and uncomfortable with each other. We feel Martin is able to make the relevance clear somehow."

"It's a lot to face up to. I was feeling earlier that there is almost a fatal attraction between the over-male woman and the over-feminine man – it's like an atomic bomb waiting to go off. It's sort of fission or fusion, whichever it is. They come together and there is a most enormous bang."

"Absolutely. Now let's see it energetically in terms of fire and water. What is happening? The woman is raising fire in her being, isn't she? And the man is feeling awash in some way that isn't good. He isn't feeling in control of that awashness, is he? It's so tidal; it's like the emotions. The emotional pull is absolutely imperative and there is a feeling of tidal water coming over men right now. It is very difficult, we suggest, for men to stay on their feet almost, while women are getting more and more fiery. It has sort of taken off in some roller-blade way that is making everyone more extreme now.

"May we suggest, then, that the premonition is of fire and water running away from each other and separating into two runaway elemental forces. The only answer, perhaps, is to recognise something of enormous importance – Q for Quan Yin."

Q for Quan Yin

Quan Yin is an energy field that, in our view, can bring a level of integration between masculine and feminine energies into manifestation on the planet now. Quan Yin is, always has been, and always will be the over-lighting energy of China, and for that reason we suggest China has a great role to play in the future manifestation of Quan Yin's real purpose.

Quan Yin is the ultimate feminine energy; the energy of the Soul of God. In fact, Quan Yin was designated a male Boddisatva in the Indian culture, before becoming feminised by Chinese mythology as the Goddess of Mercy. In fact Quan Yin has over-lighted China for 15,000 years.

We feel the energy in China has, of course, become tainted. When a feminine energy is over-stimulated by maleness it becomes fascist in texture, with that cleverness of mind that happens to female energy. Mind control and mind games can really affect the people involved and we suggest there have been more control games played in China over the last century than ever before in human existence.

The amount of mind game control displayed in China is about the feminine energy overwhelmed by male fascist input. And yet, if we assume that in planetary terms the renewed feminine energy of Quan Yin is able to manifest deeply in the psyche of humanity, then China clearly can expect to play a role in this huge realignment of the feminine that is happening now. The re-emergence of the feminine will in turn allow a new masculine energy to emerge on the planet.

Quan Yin energy is beginning to be experienced by those women who have taken responsibility for their journey into feminine spirituality and new womanhood. They have encompassed a level of animus energy within themselves and recognised their inner male of consciousness, knowing all along that this is not the whole story. They have gone on to an exploration of femininity that has allowed them to recognise an even deeper level of womanhood; one that is neither the original 'anima' woman, in touch with instinctual levels of feminine nature, nor the animus-driven woman who found herself a more equal place on the planet.

This profound level of the feminine, anchored at the heart of the matter in the Soul, is the 'woman in white'. She is able to experience Quan Yin in a very deep manner indeed and it is the energy of Quan Yin that will be mediated to the male, in order for him to make his own changes now.

*   *   *

"May we suggest Martin can tell us what Quan Yin energy feels like. In fact it is not very easy to distinguish. Life goes on, yet it remains the same. In some ways the new kind of woman still has the earlier kinds of woman deeply ingrained in her: the anima woman and the animus-infused woman. What is the extra quality that becomes apparent when these two kinds of women are integrated within a 'woman in white', Martin?"

"What I can see – it's almost like a line, a vertical line of whiteness going through the body of the woman. It's like a column going through and it seems it is white and it is of fiery material, almost. It's a fiery vibration."

"Go on. This is what we feel can be experienced alongside the rest of the woman, yes? It's a finer vibration that is energising the woman because she has taken responsibility for the consciousness of becoming a real woman now. Tell us how this white light works, Martin? This is an integration, isn't it, of fire and water at some level? How is that feeling, Martin?"

"It doesn't appear to be a light from above but more a balancing between above and below ... it's between Heaven and Earth. It's like

a compact cylinder which is part of the human being, to put it in physical terms, but it's not a shaft of light coming from the Heavens and it's not just coming up from Earth; it's very much contained between the two."

"Absolutely. May we ask Martin to feel the equality of what we call Soul energy. Soul energy is what mediates between Heaven and Earth. The Soul is within the human being who has made it their job to integrate Heaven and Earth within at a very deep level. And in the 'woman in white' there is such a feeling. Describe the woman who has found her Soul. Describe Quan Yin to us. Describe the Soul of God to us. The Soul of God is inside the integrated woman, we suggest. And what is that, Martin, in energy terms?"

"It feels tremendously practical."

"Go on."

"The build-up you gave it almost made it impossible to say what it was, but when you touch into it... it has a quality of ordinariness that is very magnificent; special."

"Absolutely. Go on. More about its quality of experience too."

"Yes. In some ways I think it's probably unnoticeable because although it is very experienced it has an innocence about it; it's almost approaching things afresh. It certainly isn't 'been there, done that, got the T-shirt' at all, because it does have an innocence. But it's an innocence which is coated by ..."

"Wisdom?"

"Maybe just an understanding. I don't think it is wisdom because I think wisdom in the old sense is knowing, but it's not knowing, it's understanding."

"Absolutely. There is no charge emotionally, is there? It just is, and in some ways, when people say 'I did the dishes, then got enlightenment and then did the dishes', it's like that, isn't it? There's no charge, so it faces life in the now moment, afresh and innocent. But the effect on others is what? The effect on the partner is what, Martin? In some ways surprising, because enlightenment isn't that flash of spiritual thunder, is it? What is the energetic effect of the Soul-infused woman?"

"I think it could be very confusing for a partner who hasn't taken his life in hand. Because the simplicity of it would call into question, in a realistic way, all the perquisites of life that surround us at that particular moment. So it could be very challenging, I think, for a partner who isn't crawling along the same tunnel."

"Absolutely. There is so much in this innocence that challenges the partner and other people in the environment, of course. Because if someone is offering nothing at some level, but offering innocence and understanding at another level, then the whole energetic framework of the other person starts jangling and feeling uncomfortable. Because the innocence is calling the energetic shifts needed, yes?"

"And how."

"Absolutely. And how."

R for Retribution

The way we see it is that many people are in denial of the necessity to understand the idea of retributive karma at this stage. Not everyone has been able to understand that they carry negative patterning from humanity's complex journey through history – as well as from their own personal journey through aeons and aeons of time since first they landed on planet Earth.

We feel there needs to be a recognition of how retribution works, and an understanding of how life will have to operate in the next ten years or so, for people who have not so far allowed their inner discomfort to become conscious. A time is coming when the emotionality of humanity will not be felt in the same way. As Earth raises its vibrations, the karmic, retributive experience will not be available in the same way.

May we suggest, therefore, that karmic history needs to be understood within every human being now, in order for life to move forward – not only on planet Earth, but within the universal unfolding plan.

Each individual until now has brought with him into incarnation an original wound – a Soul wound, the effect of our Fall from Grace, if you like – which needs to be recognised and released in the now moment of time. We have talked at length about this before.* There are five basic wound patterns which underpin life to a greater or lesser extent and at times of crisis can be overwhelming. Through series of lifetimes we have operated negatively out of these wounds through fear. The wounds are rejection, abuse, denial, abandonment and betrayal.

We feel Martin has recognised some very difficult and unpleasant patterning from karmic history, which has indeed dovetailed with his own experiences in this life. Martin's own patterning has been predominantly about rejection, and at some level he knows that for much of his life he saw rejection within every context he found himself in.

Of course, each individual creates his own story and the journey of each person's relationship to their woundedness looks different. Martin, in his fear of rejection, manifested a sensitivity to feeling disregarded. Annie, whose wound was also rejection, responded with a fear of being unsafe on the planet, compounded all her life by a sense of isolation.

We are suggesting that everyone carries a Soul wound that affects their behaviour in this life and that each person sees out of their 'window of woundedness'. When the wound has been recognised and released, scar tissue will remain, and it will itch occasionally. The memories are there to remind you of the wound, but it is to recognise and pass on. The wound remains the engine of the being, but, in its realignment it is ready to serve rather than hinder.

"Can Martin tell us what retributive karma becomes when it turns into what we call redemptive karma?"

"I think it's an awareness every time it pops up. You see it and you say 'Ooh, I know I could feel disregarded here'. But immediately you recognise it and say 'But it's not me, it's fine, I understand the situation', and you stand back.

"An acknowledgement of the wound, I think, enables you to see it in other people. It's very painful because you know what they're going through day by day, that the mind-set is overtaken by this certainty of whatever it is they see in the situation. We are programmed to take things on board exactly as we need to perceive them for our wound. No more and no less."

"Absolutely. But more than that, Martin. What is the fuel for your own life now – particularly in relationship – from that retributive to redemptive karmic situation? In other words, the relationship must have weathered the karmic difficulties of rejection and now there is the opportunity to make it part of the relationship in a positive manner? In a larger way, Martin, what does the release of karmic patterning do, in the sense of allowing worldly patterns to shift now, and what is that in terms of relationship?"

"Well, I realise that over the last however many lifetimes, and certainly in this life, I have been victim to every situation. Any relationship I've been in, I have seen myself at some level, in some way, a victim of the other person or circumstance. I suppose a broader view would be that we are victims of civilisation.

"Certainly in the West all you hear on television is people spilling their heart out because they are victim to their situation, or to the State, or the lack of funding; to this, to that, or whatever. But maybe that is now up for grabs. We can now move on from all being victims and take control of our own circumstances and see that we are in charge of ourselves and our relationships, and our relationship to the rest of the citizens of the UK, if you like. We could all move on."

"Absolutely. There is a sense that victim consciousness has to go, and by recognising the woundedness in all our patterning, we are able to let go the sense that we are being done unto. We can stop allowing ourselves to perceive life through our woundedness.

"May we ask one last thing about what relationships can do when each person recognises and lets go their need to project all this woundedness onto others – which is also what happens in the wider context of civilisation, with nations blaming nations? If relationships can lead the way by partners not projecting their woundedness onto each other, what is the possibility for the rest of humanity?"

"All I can feel is an integrity about each individual, and the safety of each individual means that they are free to be themselves."

"Absolutely. The way the law works is that when a person is no longer victim to the outside world in the old way, he or she feels safe on the planet. This allows safety in a free-flowing relationship to another, and through that a free-flowing relationship to the rest of the world they inhabit."

---

* 'Making the Most of the Life You've Got: a manual for the New Millennium' – book plus two audio cassettes, published by Rowan Communications Ltd.

S for Spirituality

We feel the way forward is now to recognise the upliftment that can happen out of sexuality and the sense that once man has understood the patterning within himself, he can then recognise a new level of sexuality.

"We established in the last chapter that Martin's wound was rejection. For much of his life he saw disregard at every turn. May we ask Martin to see inside the old sexual metaphor, if you like, that manifests in a man who is under the patterning of disregard. What could the man in rejection feel in his manner of approach to the female, as it were?"

"I think that man would be looking for rejection at every moment."

"Now, may we ask Martin to look into the being of a man who feels abandoned at the core of his being. What would he need sexually, in some way, to remind him of his abandonment?"

"Would it be that an abandoned person would be looking for the companion that fulfils his need not to be abandoned? He is looking to hold on to someone so desperately that – I suppose in the reverse of that – he'll be looking at every moment for a sign of abandonment. He knows at the deepest level that he will always be abandoned, because that's the pattern."

"Absolutely. But, in the sexual mode of approach, what would these two men be looking for – in the sexuality itself, as it were? The rejected man looks for sexual prowess in himself, doesn't he? While the abandoned man looks for sexual mothering. Is that making sense, Martin? So may we suggest that sexuality is a needs-based preoccupation for anyone.

"Feel into the woman who has a rejection wound – who doesn't feel safe, for example. She will put sexuality into a completely different arena. In her needs-based sexuality she wants safety, but to lose herself in sexuality is not feeling safe at all, so she will manifest a frigidity in some way. The woman with the abandonment wound will feel the need to merge with her partner and is then unable to distinguish between herself and her man, until he abandons her and then she is in total disarray.

"May we suggest this also concerns wounds of betrayal, abuse and denial. We all operate sexually out of our wounds, as well in our emotional day-to-day life. It is quite a business to become aware of our woundedness and then to recognise our sexuality as a relationship between one wound or another.

"In a relationship there must be an understanding of woundedness. Partners can recognise within themselves their own woundedness and learn how not to operate out of these wounds sexually or otherwise. Our own relationship to the human race is not about making anyone be anything they don't want to be. But raising this issue of woundedness now, in order to offer people the opportunity to become very different human beings, is part of our mission to explain. Relationships need to flourish, sexually as well as spiritually, and it is clear why sexuality needs to be addressed in a different manner now.

"We feel the way forward, then, is to re-cap on some of the difficulties of a relationship where one partner is wounded in one way and the other is wounded in another – which, as we say, is everyman's journey one way or another. So, Martin, in order to move sexuality away from what many people experience as a quagmire of insecurity, feel the difficulty in approach somehow."

"The image I have is of a knight on a horse, in full armour, approaching a fair lady. But, unfortunately, he's going off to the north and she's facing south-east, so they can never see each other.

"There is no way that they can ever see or meet each other for what they truly are. There is a sense of desperateness about the quest to get themselves together, because they are both seeing different pictures."

"Absolutely. In the woundedness, the sexuality isn't in the same ball-park at any level, is it Martin? So each one is wanting their wounds addressed, if not dressed in the situation, and there is no coming together. Even if people are having a 'wowee' sexual time, they are not in touch with each other at a deep level, are they?"

"I think if they take a moment to feel into it, or discuss it at some level, they are both going to be dissatisfied with what the other is saying. As you say, they are in a different ball-park."

"Absolutely. And now, if Martin is able to make a leap of faith here, look into a more whole relationship which is totally clear of the depth of woundedness that takes place between two sexual beings. What is the relationship about then, Martin, sexually and spiritually together?"

"It's about confluence; about being more comfortable. There is a sense of joy about the sexuality and it's closely aligned to spirituality. It's so close to spirituality that at some level they are almost indistinguishable."

"There is a coming together in a profoundly new way, isn't there? In what way is this profound new coming together relevant now?"

"I feel that this is an age of choice, and I feel both parties have a choice to enter into their relationship. They can choose to find a spirituality through their sexuality, as well as in other areas of their life. But it's not a knight's sexuality, but it is a quest for spirituality."

"Absolutely. There is within two human beings a merging into a higher third, isn't there, at some level? What happens in that higher third, Martin?"

"Higher third sounds a very musical connotation but I think that's probably the right metaphor for it. It's something which is a very beautiful vibration of sound. It's akin to a wonderful orchestral piece or whatever musically is your epitome of joy and spirituality, then that's what is obtainable."

"Absolutely."

T for Twelve

"May we suggest Martin is able to tell us why twelve is relevant to this book right now. There is a sense that twelve is a critical number and in our view, twelve will be a very important number in the future. Why number twelve?"

"I suppose that it must resonate with the new energy, the new dimension of reality."

"Absolutely. There is a numerical relationship between twelve and the way the human being will operate in the new age of mankind, yes? What is the feeling?"

"Oh yes. Could this be about DNA?"

"Absolutely. There are twelve strands of DNA in the unfolding evolutionary process of the fullness of mankind now."

"And we only have two; is it two?"

"Absolutely. We are in the moment of transition now. In the coming era of unfolding evolutionary materiality within human beings, there is an upgrading of the DNA spiral towards the twelve strands of DNA that mankind had before 'the flood'. And, in our view, it is the flood that we are repairing, if you like, in order for mankind to become twelve-stranded DNA material beings again.

"And in that growth of the DNA strand we are absolutely sure that man will recognise himself as a great being again, in order to take responsibility once more, not only for his own manifestation, but also for planetary evolutionary unfolding. It was this understanding that mankind was aware of at the beginning of time, but which in some way was 'unravelled' at a later stage. It is now 're-ravelling' into his awareness at a new level, in a new way. Indeed, it is a recognition that mankind is the key to his own unfolding now. Mankind can now become a new material being, within whom is a spiritual divinity that creates God on Earth for all time.

"But we want Martin to feel into before the flood now, and tell us what that feeling was. What was it that created a need for the animals to go in two by two; to stay in the way God wished them to stay, until the flood was over? What is the feeling that happened inside mankind before the flood?"

"It's almost as if those incarnating at that time were aware of their divinity. I'm seeing a perspective of Earth, of people arriving on Earth, knowing they were God-like. They arrived on Earth almost with the full knowledge of themselves."

"What does that feel like, Martin, to have a full knowledge that they are God's children on Earth, somehow?"

"Well, it feels like two things. One of being emissaries and therefore not Earth people per se. And the second is that it's impossible to forget who you are, so it's difficult to play out the role that you have been given on Earth. You are always aware that you are only acting on a stage and it seems as though the change, the DNA change when it came, was a loss of memory.

"The 'two by two' is a metaphor for the two-stranded DNA; that the two by two animals going in is very much the two strands of DNA. The DNA had to be reduced for man to forget his divinity for a while. To go forward into the future of Earth we had to become simpler beings; to become real Earth people."

"Absolutely. There was a need for the divine Sun beings to mate with the Earth beings in order for evolution to be played out. Before the memory loss, there was a sort of stage-acting about life on Earth in this regard. A loss of memory was absolutely necessary for the divine beings to mate wholly and completely with Earth man. Mankind needed to become a hybrid being for the task ahead; that of becoming a more integrated cosmic being on Earth, for Earth's task to be completed. And in that completion, Earth had then to know its significance in the scheme of things.

"So mankind lost its memory of being divine and the two by two-stranded DNA creature went ahead and, in the unfolding, made itself a creature of Earth. Now, in the next years of the new millennium, there will be a gradual remembering, because men and women are recognising again the divinity within themselves, on Earth. There will be a recognition that a twelve-strand DNA man, is God in Earth. How does that feel now, Martin?"

"It feels very different from the beings who set out from the cosmos to arrive on Earth. It almost feels as though, in some ways, they were knowing beings coming to Earth. The twelve-stranded beings, who will be on Earth, will be much more innocent."

"So may we suggest the evolutionary process has been for humanity to lose its memory. Then for beings on Earth to begin again to become conscious, only to lose their memory once more to recognise their divinity. It is complex, isn't it, but there is a real recognition that the memory of consciousness is returning to prepare for another loss of memory because there needs to be an understanding inside the being and not a memory of the being.

"There are so many wheels within wheels and in our view the remembering is happening at such a rapid pace. And yet, the memories also need to be let go, in order simply for man to be man in his divine being on Earth. We feel Martin can tell us what the outcome is, in some way that is wondrous for mankind in his twelve-strand materiality now."

"It feels like a far greater connection with the cosmos. An understanding of the cosmos which we have struggled with blindly,

uncomprehendingly, scientifically. And suddenly we will just know it."

"Mankind will just understand cosmic dimensions within himself, in the sense that he will have all the dimensions within him, won't he? He will remember himself as a divine being, and then forget himself again because, in the remembering there will be understanding that it is as it is, as it is. It's the next stage, isn't it? To forget once again and simply understand it all, in some way."

"And there is a sense that the fear of letting go the knowing is balanced by input such as this (guidance), which gives us what we need to know. It's a feeling that there will always be input which is appropriate to the situation."

"Absolutely. We are part of a wider dimensional relationship to humanity and it is simply a level of information that is available within the human being who has the courage to let go everything that is not, in essence, the human being. That's a paradox indeed. What does that mean, Martin, to courageously let go being human in order to be a fuller human being?"

"I suppose to be human, at the moment, is to be very mindful. That is what is considered the epitome of achievement as a human being, to be clever – full of intellectual information. To allow that to go must be, for most people caught up in the academic tradition of the West, the greatest sacrifice. And I suppose, to move forward, we have to let that go and allow this information to be accessed at a different level in a different world."

"That's a real test, isn't it, to let go information and reach out for understanding?"

U for Understanding

May we suggest that in the coming years, the way to recognise information will not be through the intellectual mind anymore. There will be more a sense of imbibing information in such a way that life will be understood; not manifestly recognised and then analysed into pieces.

The scientific mode has been to separate out things that are recognised and analysed for content. That's the way science works. But, in our view, what needs to happen in the coming years is to collect information from the material by absorbing it; accessing it through the being, rather than seeing something, separating it off from its whole and analysing it.

There is so much analysis of everything that everyone is dependent for analysis on scientists, and then we are told what to do according to the analysis. But, in our view, the beef crisis, for example, isn't about analysing bone or beef but more about recognising why the situation has arisen and then making sure it doesn't happen again.

There is a mode of accessing information that bypasses the brain, that allows each individual, and not only the person with a brilliant brain, to know and understand things and act upon their understanding. The human being is shifting gear so profoundly. There won't be such dependence on the intellectual, academic brain that analyses, remembers and casts aside the whole for the part.

"We feel Martin is able to feel the way the brain does its analysis. Martin is not much of an analytical person at all, but he can recognise how analysis is created by separating the parts from the whole. What is the feeling in the brain itself, somehow?"

"It feels like it wants to sub-divide out into little ... into cells, into the cellular level, anything that comes its way."

"Absolutely. The brain separates into little cells, which is how information gets separated and analysed. What is analysis about then, as the cells are separated out and examined analytically?"

"It feels like attempting to understand and grade each individual part according to its work."

"Absolutely. There is a sense of creating worth by separation, isn't there? And it is worth that is the key here. If you recognise how people separate and analyse and grade and decide upon the worth of a single cell even, that isn't how people can feel self-worth, is it Martin? Why not?"

"Self-worth feels like ... much more connected to the integrity of the whole."

"The integrity of the whole creates a sense of worth somehow, doesn't it? You don't analyse and separate out to feel self-worth, but consider the value of the whole being, not discarding bits that aren't up to standard even, because that is how fascism arrives.

"There is a fascism in science, in fact, that must separate out and decide on worth as a mechanism for living. We feel that is why Martin is not able to be naturally analytical, is he? What's the sense you have of not being analytical, and yet, of course, often feeling unworthy because you don't work in the analytical framework?"

"I somehow can't see things in that way. I don't quite know why."

"Why not? Why can't you separate out in this way? What's happening inside you that won't allow you to separate things out in this manner, in the way the brain person can?"

"I knew this would come into it. I heard a radio programme about the discovery of the quark, last night, and it struck me that for every level of enquiry, a new particle would appear. It was almost as if

science could provide for these people's searching. One more level and then they'll find another beyond that. Every time something was found, someone had predicted it six months before it happened. And then they found it."

"Absolutely. That is exactly how it works, because we create our own reality, in some ways. But tell us what Martin feels because he cannot think analytically and in some ways he's felt unworthy because he can't think analytically."

"But it all seems so pointless to me."

"Why? What's the sense of the analytical mind, that you don't find appealing?"

"It doesn't see the value of anything."

"Absolutely. May we suggest the analytical mind only makes patterns, it doesn't make value of what it sees. There is no need to keep making patterns, is there Martin? Because that's what needs to disappear, at some level, to create something else as the marker point for value. What is that feeling like, Martin? What creates value in your understanding, right now?"

"Could it be something in the individual elements, which are analysed individually. I don't see them having an effect on my life. If I analysed an onion, it wouldn't have any effect on the onion as an integral whole; it is something which looks good in the garden, which I can eat and enjoy. There's so much to an onion; it makes me cry, it has many, many layers, it's such a good metaphor for life.

"I don't need to get under the onion's skin to understand it – to understand the way it operates. Is this the problem? For example, people are trying to understand the nitty-gritty of organics without actually seeing the overview which is energetic; the effect that

organic gardening has on the gardener and the recipient of the food; the wholeness of it."

"Absolutely. The way most people study is to analyse things in detail – particularly in English Literature – they pull apart something that is beautiful and create a very unbeautiful relationship to it, because there is so little receptivity to the content.

"We feel that is the way things happen a lot in life and, of course, the way women have found consciousness has led to more analysis by women. But by doing so they are moving away from their femininity. Martin has a great deal of femininity in him, which absorbs life in a more whole way. But many women who have made the male inside them stronger, have taken over the analysis function from the men and are, as we said before, even better at it.

"But, in fact, understanding rather than recognising and separating is manifestly more valuable now for women. Through the receiving of life; through the making valuable of all life, it is possible to understand all that is and all that is within themselves.

"We feel Martin is able to recognise that he has a feminine being, which is able to absorb life more than Annie does at some level, and this absorbing life is his marker point for life now. What does this mean for the woman now? The one who no longer knows it all; the one who can no longer tell you how the universe works, even from her own experience?"

"It feels like a pointer on a dial, rather like a 'swingometer'. You sweep the dial and the more you sweep away from the analytical, the more you get into receptivity. As the analytical goes down the receptivity is able to increase. They are both ends of the same piece of string almost."

"Of course women had to be influenced by their inner male. The inner male is consciousness par excellence and in our view many

women now have an extremely well-integrated male side which
they have used to know things at a very profound level. But at
another turn of the spiritual, letting go all she knows consciously,
by releasing everything she has known up to now, the woman is
able to perceive, receive and make known far more about the way
things are.

"To become an understander rather than a knower requires the
letting go of all knowing. After that intense needing to know, there
can be a profound releasing of what is known, from what is
understood in life. May we suggest Martin can tell us what he
knows now, that Annie doesn't know, about her life's work – once
she totally releases the need to know best, which comes from her
experience of knowing so much."

*"It may be a diversion, but I got the joke. For the period since the
flood we've held Noah's Ark to be the sort of central core. I think
the 'Un-Noah's' Ark is now the place for people!"*

"Into unknowing!"

*"Yes, into unknowing. I wonder if that might mean you can lead
them twelve by twelve!"*

"May we also suggest that Annie will finally experience the peace
that passes all understanding, which the analytical brain simply has
no idea of. That's the key to the peace that passes all understanding,
isn't it, Martin?"

*"I think if I hadn't been needing to tell you my joke, I might have
got there. Sorry, I got distracted!"*

V for Vermin

We want to recognise the way animals play their part in the situation between men and women now. That's quite a thought, isn't it? That whatever animal comes into the environment, makes a statement about relationships. We feel Martin and Annie will smile at this, considering their mole problem and the fact that Annie saw a mouse in the house the other day.

"We feel Martin is able now to feel the way the moles have mirrored the relationship between Martin and Annie, over the last year. Why have the moles just gone on proliferating? In such a way that now the whole lawn is a mole tunnel. We feel the way forward is to ask Martin to recognise how the moles tunnel, in some way?"

"Blindly going forward in search of worms."

"Blindly moving forward to get enough nourishment to exist, and there is a lot of food in the environment to keep at it. Why is there enough food there, Martin, to nourish them?"

"Plenty of worms."

"Absolutely. Plenty of nourishment in the environment, isn't there? But they keep going on and on in the tunnelling mode, don't they? They annoy Martin and Annie, who don't want to get rid of them by gassing them, but wish they would disappear because they are not making a lawn to be proud of, are they? What is the feeling, then, about all this business in the environment that is extremely nourishing?"

"Is there something that we have to do ...or they have to do?"

"Absolutely. They need to keep tunnelling, don't they? To make themselves more and more nourished, in some way. They are, in fact, very happy moles in the environment, aren't they? Because there is so much nourishment. They don't know you're annoyed with them, tunnelling under the entire lawn. What is the feeling, Martin, about the way the moles are just going on and on and on in the situation, without recognising how much it inconveniences you?"

"They are oblivious, aren't they? I think they're just on a different level, have no consciousness of us whatsoever, at some level. Obviously they know humans are around, but once they get their heads down they have to be what they have to be."

"Absolutely. Why in Martin and Annie's lawn is there such good nourishment, perhaps? Why does Martin call the moles to his environment in such profusion? To do with his need to keep taking more and more nourishment from the environment, without recognising his mode of gathering nourishment isn't necessary really, because there's always more. He keeps tunnelling and tunnelling and tunnelling, doesn't he, to get more nourishment from the environment somehow? What's the feeling around that, Martin?"

"Is there a desperation about it?"

"Absolutely. What has this got to do with letting go the umbilical cord now, to become very separate from Annie at some level. To become less dependent on the need for nourishment to be provided perhaps."

"Superficially, they do seem to be opposites. If you are having your nourishment provided, you don't need to compulsively go and dig, do you?"

"Absolutely. What's the feeling about the moles keeping on keeping on, in this manic manner? Is there some connection here with Martin's old way of needing to keep tunnelling for his nourishment, now?"

"It's not something I really recognise. I know the compulsiveness, but I'm not ..."

"May we suggest Martin feels into how the moles keep tunnelling for more and more worms, in an environment that is not lacking in nourishment. They don't actually need to do all this manic gathering of worms, because there is plenty there for them in one burrow, as it were. What is the feeling of manic gathering for nourishment that is everywhere available, anyway? Can Martin feel what's happening to the moles that resonates to his own fears, perhaps, at some level?"

"So, I've attracted moles who have the same worries that I do, manic need? Or have I attracted the animal that does that manicly? Do all moles ...?"

"Absolutely."

"Yes, so you attract the animal that is appropriate to what you do?"

"Absolutely."

"It must be very difficult if you attract elephants!"

"May we suggest that's exactly as it happens, Martin. Feel yourself manicly trying to get nourishment from the environment that is full of nourishment. Does that make sense to part of Martin's psyche that was quite fearful about being nourished in the relationship, at some level that Martin can recognise?"

"I suppose the thing that I do recognise is the need to grow a lot of food which is the manifestation of that situation. I find it more difficult to get to grips with the underlying ..."

"Let's look at it more closely, then. The way Martin wants to do everything in excess to get more food than is necessary is a symptom of this fear that there won't be enough. Can Martin resonate to that?"

"Mm."

"Annie has the opposite reaction to the same difficulty that there won't be enough. Does that make sense?"

"Yes, totally."

"Both Martin and Annie were fearful that there wouldn't be enough, and Martin has the need to keep making it all right by having excess in some way. Does that make sense, Martin?"

"Mm."

"Feel that in the relationship now."

"Yes, I suppose it's an abundance of love, isn't it, of feeling an abundance of affection."

"Martin kept wanting more proof, didn't he, even when Annie was showering him with her way of loving. There was a need for proof of the lovingness to nourish him. And yet, he felt there wasn't enough of it and he kept pushing and pushing to prove there was enough love. Does that make sense?

"So the moles represent all this tunnelling, more and more and more, when there's plenty in the environment. Martin has an abundant amount of love pouring into him. Can he feel that? It's in the environment, all round. And yet he kept tunnelling for more. Yes? That's all the moles are representing, does that make sense?"

"Mm."

"May we suggest Martin is able now to recognise how the moles can be told to disappear, now, in the recognition that they have?"

"Will they take their tunnels away, that's the question?"

"May we suggest that it is Martin's task to re-do the lawn. But how will he tell the moles to disappear, now that he knows he's got enough love in his environment to last a lifetime?"

"I suppose you just tell them!"

"Absolutely. They can understand you, can't they? You just needed to get to the point where you don't need them to show you it's all there, if you just knew it. And that's vermin in the highest sense of the word, isn't it?

"Vermin are representatives of the unconscious, Martin, aren't they, in this regard? And vermin are called vermin because people don't like them at all. Because they make people recognise themselves as they truly are, and that's not a very good task, is it?

"We feel the mouse is quite harmless, of course, and has disappeared now. But we feel Martin is able to tell Annie why she saw a mouse nibbling away in front of her in the hall, and it simply stayed there – not scampering around much – in front of her. What was this telling Annie at some level?"

"There's an air of confidence about the mouse, isn't there?"

"It was very confident, yes."

"Perhaps it just felt comfortable."

"Absolutely. May we suggest the mouse was confidently making itself felt in the environment and, in some ways, Annie is now making herself felt in her environment. It's about some incredible shyness in Annie disappearing enough to allow her to stand her ground, no matter how much she feels afraid. May we suggest that the mouse isn't in the house any more, it just needed to tell Annie she is able to stand up – unafraid – now, in the face of what might seem a hugely terrifying experience.

"We feel the flies in the lampshades are also a message. What is the message, Martin, about the relationship now? Those flies are irritants, aren't they? And Martin and Annie do find irritants in the relationship, but they are dying out now, as these flies are dying out. What is the feeling then, about the flies and about the irritating noise in the lampshades?"

"My feeling about them is that I could kill them if I wanted, but I don't like to kill them, I don't like to kill things. Speaks volumes, doesn't it?"

" About your irritations, Annie's irritations?"

"Our irritations. I obviously don't quite want to get rid of them."

"Absolutely. May we suggest that flies don't have feelings. They aren't really animals in the sense of how we regard animals and insects. The flies are a real anachronism in evolutionary terms and we feel they can be disposed of. So, irritations can be got rid of, Martin, no shame, no blame. They aren't required any more in the situation. It's not in the dimension Martin and Annie now inhabit. Irritations are passé in the relationship. May we ask Martin what he feels about vermin indicators, now."

"I think they're terribly useful."

"May we suggest the reason vermin come into a book on relationships, is that indeed relationships have vermin-like qualities, from time to time, and in our view, what needs to be recognised is that indeed we call vermin to us in such a way that we can find ourselves recognising some parts of our unconscious processes.

"We feel the owl, for example, which all people love at some level, has a story to tell when it isn't just a wonderful creature of the night. How does the owl speak to the unconscious, if someone has an encounter with an owl, that is a little frightening perhaps. What is their business about? What is the message of an owl, perhaps?"

"The only time I've come across an owl, I was shocked by its beauty, but, I think there was a fear there. I was quite afraid."

"In what way afraid? It is stunningly beautiful, of course, but how might it speak to Martin's fear level? What does the owl represent, as it were, in relationship terms? What could have been happening in the situation then?"

"It was a time of great difficulty, great disturbance and at a time of great unhappiness."

"Absolutely. What was the owl telling you then, Martin, at this time of great fear, about a beautiful creature? Indeed, who was the beautiful creature shall we wonder?"

"I think, in all modesty, it was probably me."

"Oh, do you?"

"Mm."

"Absolutely. And the terror?"

"Me, too, I should think."

"Absolutely. The owl is darkness and light, together, and at some level Martin was recognising the light and therefore throwing up a darkness within himsclf, at the same time."

"What I actually did was, I was so fascinated by the owl that I kept shining my torch on it, and eventually it flew away. So I can see the 'deep and meaningful' of that totally. But it was stunningly beautiful, and it was in our tree."

"So people call vermin omens. There is a negative aspect to an omen. At the same time, there is a possibility of redeeming the symbol, as it were. May we suggest, for example, Annie had a snake across her doorway in Stroud. That was an omen in some way. What was the omen about, Martin?"

"Could it be an opening?"

"Absolutely. An opening with difficulty, in some way. We feel these omens are placed for the individual to read."

W for Warrior

We would make the point here that the 'warrior woman' is now on the way out as we have suggested. We feel the warrior woman was the woman who became more male than the male, and it is time for a new perspective on femaleness. A very different perspective from the woman who knew it all, suddenly, who could do it all, suddenly, and who felt they should do it all, suddenly.

No one is denying how much women have achieved in the last thirty years, and indeed no one would put the clock back . We sense evolution stamps forward in its incredible manner and, in the scheme of things, time is now speeding on and on at a much faster rate. So, there is a crescendo towards the moment when time stops again, in some way, that needs to be understood and indeed experienced by mankind now.

There is a sense of speeding up in time, that creates fear and confusion in many people, who simply don't recognise themselves from day to day. There are people who feel they have been left behind on some sort of scrap heap because they cannot keep up with all the technology, for example. Many people who cannot work the technology feel they aren't in the run of life any longer, because more and more is demanded of them. And so time speeds on and on and on. And in the end, we suggest, time itself cannot speed on beyond Earth's own timing in evolutionary terms.

We feel that time is now pliable, in many people's experience. Indeed the idea that life can be re-run is gradually becoming more acceptable. Past lives are accessible to many people now, and what is that, if not making time pliable? We suggest, too, that future time is now available. So there must be something happening to time itself within the psyche of humanity.

We sense the warrior woman is a woman who acknowledges time to be extremely important. The warrior woman looks at the time, all the time, because there is so little time to operate all those parts of herself. Indeed, she never has enough time for anything but chasing time. And, in our view, this is the crunch point. It has to stop, this running out of time feeling, because, in fact, time itself is a mirage. Time isn't real, and therefore to be ruled by time is not allowing man to be real at his deepest level. It is only being a personality chasing time.

*   *   *

"We feel Martin can tell us how the warrior woman chases time in an inappropriate manner. Because she is the one who has reached the pinnacle of timeliness to change the attitude to time."

"I think what first came to mind was the biological clock – the biological imperative. To get a career in and produce children and do everything else. There seem to be inbuilt marker points."

"Absolutely."

Time is a marker-point situation, so women are time-keepers, par excellence. But in that time-keeping, the warrior woman has become the time maker not the time marker as such. There needs to be a recognition that time needs to be reperceived now, particularly by the warrior woman, because unless she reperceives time, her biological clock will pack up anyway. We feel many women are unable to conceive now, because timing is very inner not outer, and if the warrior woman over-rides her inner timing, then she will never be able to conceive in her time. It's as simple as that.

We feel a real need now for the warrior woman to stop running ahead of time and to become aware that she needs to recognise feminine timing now – not masculine timing, which is far more directional in some ways. Female timing is more cyclical, it is more in touch with cyclical, rhythmical time than male timing. And if the woman loses her cyclical timing mechanism, she can't be a true woman anymore.

That is quite a threat but, in our view, warrior women are likely to come a cropper, because operating out of such directed maleness must make itself felt in the world. We are unable to continue the relationship to Earth, unless the cyclical nature of Earth is worked with and conducted in the correct way.

It is the woman's place now to reperceive her own timing and to let go the maleness she has acquired in the process of becoming conscious. There is indeed a new womanliness required now, in order for the planet to re-establish quality of timing that is being lost as the world hurtles on and on and on.

"Can Martin feel the necessity for women to stop hurtling in some way, so that the world can stop spinning in a way that makes everyone feel out of control?"

"It feels as if the woman's role is to be a fixed point. I think the male is meant to zoom around a bit, with male energy, but the woman is much more a ..."

"An anchor, an anchorite?"

"An anchorite, yes."

"What does the anchorite feel like, Martin? In some way that creates a feeling of stability in the world, now?"

"Strangely, the anchorite seems to have her feet not just on the ground, but almost in the ground. It's very connected."

"Absolutely."

"So that others are connected by bonds to the anchorite. They can move about in safety."

"Absolutely. May we suggest that Martin is able to sense that a warrior woman is very unanchored to her femaleness, at some level, in the Earth plane. More and more women are recognising a need to descend into the Earth plane. More and more women are realising the emptiness of the unanchored, speedy life now. And, of course, it is causing much anxiety and confusion because the speedy life is totally speedy and impossible to let go. It's like being on a whirligig that can't stop.

"But those who manage to get off the whirligig and make themselves really dependent on Earth again are recognising their femaleness in a new manner. How is this new woman able to stand anchored in Earth in a new way now?"

"The first thing I feel about coming off the whirligig, is that it causes a great deal of sickness and discomfort – when you first take your position on Earth. But, there's a sense of increasing confidence as you are grow in stature, as you retain your position. And looking back at the previous life I think the feeling must be one of incredible amazement that you ever did it, or needed to do it, and why it was so seductive even."

"Absolutely. What is important now, is that 'still spot' in the woman who can make herself the mediator between Heaven and Earth; who can be the anchor to men on Earth, who even find it impossible to get on the whirligig again. May we suggest that this in itself is frightening to women who find they simply don't have the means to get on the whirligig any more.

"But there is sacrifice in every move forward. Women make sacrifices – that is a feminine trait, it goes with the territory – and for every sacrifice made, there is reward in abundance. That is the way the Universe works. If anyone gives up something they passionately want to continue doing, because the patterning is dictating that they should, then they are rewarded by a higher level of experience.

"We feel Martin is able, then, to feel relationship when the woman, the 'woman in white', is anchored in her own feminine being. What does a male want from the woman, now?"

"I think a sense of peace."

"Absolutely. The woman who is in her real, receiving, feminine mode now, will mediate the peace of God that passeth all understanding."

X for Xianzai (Now)

May we suggest China is very important in the coming millennium. Of course, America is afraid that China will usurp its position economically, and they are correct. China will become a massive economic power in the world. We feel China has an immense contribution to make, not only economically, but also spiritually. And, in our view, there needs to be an understanding of what China's energy can offer to relationship now.

Chinese spirituality has entered the West at a very significant time and, ironically, it is the West which is recognising the value of the Chinese heritage, more than the Chinese themselves. Right now they are set upon the economic path which the West began two hundred years ago. However, we feel there will come a time when it is possible for China to recognise itself as an immense contributor of spiritual vitality and that there is a recognition coming, within China itself, that it has more to contribute than mere economic strength.

We feel China will be able to re-gather its history in the same way that many individuals in the West are now consciously gathering parts of themselves, through recognition of past lives. This has become a real tool for people to access and understand parts of themselves that they simply could fathom until now, and to release them for their manifest spiritual unfolding.

We feel the Chinese recognition of yin and yang is paramount in this discovery. China has always experienced itself as carrying within it a cohesive relationship between the masculine and feminine energies. China is a cohesive nation, whether or not they have deviated from this cohesion in the past years. The Chinese Emperor was the 'Son of Heaven', and within that recognition of the 'Son of Heaven', was an inherent understanding of his relationship, as mediator and server, of the Earth.

When Chinese mandarins were the scholar class in China, their skills in art, painting, calligraphy and garden building, indicated their awareness of China as a cohesive land in itself. They recognised the cyclical nature of life on Earth and understood that man had a right and fitting place within the landscape and the cosmos. This needs to be acknowledged now and we feel the introduction of Feng Shui, Qi Gong and Chinese medicine into western culture, is symbolic of the coming recognition of man's true place within the cosmos and within the Earth itself.

"We feel Martin is able to feel what China can offer men and women in relationship right now. To begin with, the Feng Shui – the right place in the now moment of time – idea of relationship itself. In the now moment – Xianzai – relationship is as it should be, placed in the place it should be, so the now moment can unfold into the next now moment of time.

"If Martin can feel himself in his state of unfolding in the now moment, he will tell us how that feels. How does it feel to be in the right place, at the right moment, in the now time, suddenly?"

"I think it's one of feeling very relaxed."

"Why relaxed? What is the feeling that, having done all that difficult work on unconscious patterning, Martin is, right now, exactly where he should be in time and space? How does that feel?"

"It feels very pleasurable, because there is no looking behind you, over your shoulder, at past difficulties. And there is nothing to worry about. You don't need a future. You don't jump into the future all the time and sort of need to look sideways for spooks, or all the things that can go wrong. It just feels as though you are here, and that's it."

"And if Martin is in the right place at the right time and Annie is in the right place at the right time, feel how that lets you off the hook of a real sense of burden. What is the feeling, that all is for the best in the best of all possible worlds, suddenly?"

"What I'm getting is a sense of balance."

"Go on. Balance in the situation of placement of the life between Martin and Annie, now."

"It has the potential for great peace. It feels like a place of not so many words, of awaiting events really to arrive."

"Absolutely. Feel the sense, then, of the Christ Child in the manger – because this is Christmas, after all. Feel that feeling of awaiting the arrival of the shepherds, then the three Kings, the manifestation of Christ's message, if you like. What is the feeling in that awaiting the future, to be as it is to be, without fear and without making it too important even."

"What I'm getting, I don't understand – it's just recognition."

"Of?"

"The rightness of it all."

"Absolutely. Christ was born in a pretty murky place really, wasn't He? And yet it had its rightness about it. And the shepherds came, and the Kings came. What does that feel like in the sense that life needn't be perfect to create a peaceful lifestyle, without making it all so important, without having to have more, grow more, be more? This is a sense of Christ's birth, that people don't register really. What was His message in the situation He found himself in, Martin?"

"It feels like acceptance .... acceptance of the lot you've got."

"Absolutely. In that situation He accepted the life He was to lead, didn't He? That was His gift, and if the Feng Shui of each person is as it should be, then accepting life as it is, creates a now moment that can bring peace and calm, can't it? Can Martin resonate to that feeling now? What is the feeling in that acceptance of the now moment, moment by moment, in the sense of relationship?"

"There's a sort of standing still, awaiting events."

"In terms of relationship?"

"Acceptance, I think."

"What acceptance? What is the feeling as Annie stands in front of you – each person in the right place at the right time – in the now moment? How does it affect the relationship in some way that might be called new relationship? To stand still at the peaceful point, somehow."

"It feels entirely new because I think that the old form was for both partners to be absolutely tied to each other by a piece of rope, but facing outwards; both desperate to go and do their own particular thing or to exist. Either one was hanging on to the other, or running away from the other, desperately. Each party had their own axe to grind really, within the relationship. This feels like a moment in space time that is quite stationary, in some peculiar way."

"Absolutely. May we suggest there is a point in time that can be achieved in the now moment, when all is as it should be and all is right in the world of men. The peace that passeth all understanding is now – in the now moment and then all that is to be, will be in the now moment."

Y for You

'You' is about you. Each one of you is the 'You' we speak to at this moment in time. There is a sense now that each individual is recognising an enormous shift in the way the world is working. There is an unsteadiness within each individual now, about how to approach life. We sense political unsteadiness is catching, and we feel no one is quite sure, anymore, how to feel about the world.

The Conservative party in Britain is not really able to oppose, and the Labour party is absolutely struggling to remain faithful to its roots. So the rootedness of everything is shifting and changing and therefore people are feeling unsteady inside. The root is shifting and we do mean root literally. The root of the human being is changing now so that mankind is upgrading itself at a very deep level. The rootedness of man is changing profoundly.

At one level mankind is upgrading itself to a higher frequency, so the base of man is becoming lighter. At another level this actually means that man is rooting more deeply into the Earth, at a finer level, and there is a feeling of discomfort. Man's mind does not yet recognise his rootedness is inside planet Earth. He recognises it at some level, but cannot quite get it at a profound inner level.

You are the only one who can make this shift for yourself. There is no one else who can do it; not the government, not the school teacher, not the guru. Only you can recognise the shifting and make that shift inside for yourself. Not even your partner can do it for you, because the partner is a mirror for the shifting, not the medium of it. There is no one but you who can recognise what is going on inside yourself.

May we suggest that you often meet a partner in order for you to change, for you to recognise the patterning that prevents you from allowing this enormous shift to take place. The partner cannot be the ideal man on a white charger or that wonderful woman of your dreams. He or she is, in fact, almost your worst enemy, because he or she is pulled electrically into your field to show up the bits you cannot look at for yourself.

So, in these particular partnerships, there is not only love, but often hatred too. That is a tough thing to acknowledge, but if we draw our partners to us electrically in order to mirror our weaknesses, then indeed that is cause for discomfort and rage and disappointment.

No partnership is without its disappointments, especially when the partners are on the path towards their soul relationship to the divinity within. There is an attraction between those on this journey, an unconscious agreement to help each other become the person they are meant to be. The downside of this is that the partner is also the one to challenge.

Cherishing someone who is to challenge you puts you in a difficult situation. And yet, at some level it is chosen; it is correct. It is the way to become free of dependence and then, in the realisation of this independence, finally to acknowledge, recognise and understand, the interdependence of a new kind of relationship. This needs to happen if man is now to be the mediator between Heaven and Earth; between the cosmic dimensions of manifesting mind – the Universal Mind – and the increasingly conscious planet Earth, whose representative on Earth is mankind itself.

Men and women are becoming enormously skilful beings, who are able to understand how life works at infinitely complex levels of experience. The human being is a representative of the Heaven in Earth which is manifesting right now. Men and women are the chosen instruments of an unfolding Universe in time and space.

We feel the new woman, who no longer knows, is a receiver. She is by nature the receiver of inputs that come in from the cosmic dimensions. And as the receiver she allows the man to take up a new form of leadership. He recognises the inputs and uses them as a tool to lead in a very new way. Not in the old patriarchal manner of hierarchical leadership, but as a 'man of substance', who is able to recognise and understand the positioning of Heaven in Earth for himself.

As the woman mediates the inputs through her radar dish of femininity, the man will accept and recognise how Heaven manifests in Earth. It is a complex situation and it is for the future. But many, many women are now recognising their ability to receive such inputs and are witnessing that their partners, the new Earth Men, are different from the old male, who manifests life in a forceful, directional way.

"We feel Martin can tell us how the male will take up the inputs of women, like Annie, who take in the cosmic inputs at a deep level. How will he recognise Heaven in the Earth by using these inputs in a new manner of creative leadership? How will the man use the inputs from the woman's receiving mechanism?"

"It feels like sympathetically. It doesn't feel as though there's any aggressive proselytising. It feels as though there is no pushing."

"Go on. What does that mean? How do you work in the practical sense if the Earth Man is mediated by the receiving woman. How does it work, practically speaking? What do you hear from the Earth, as it were?"

"I think you hear what the Earth wants and needs. There's a sort of feeling of burgeoning need. There's a sense of the ebb and flow of the Earth that puts the whole thing into context. It's as though what Annie produces is one level, but it's almost drawing it down to Earth level and putting it into balance. There's a sense of practicality about it."

"Absolutely. Why can't the man just chat to the Earth without the woman receiving from the cosmic environment? What is the feeling of why it's happening like this? Why is the man able to talk to the Earth only because the woman has become the cosmic receiver?"

"Well, I think in the past the man could talk to the Earth, in the same way that the woman could talk to the heavens, as they did in the Temples in ancient times. But there is a sense now of getting into

balance and bringing Heaven on Earth so the two have to be combined. To bring Heaven on to Earth you have to have the two polarities bringing the whole essence into balance."

"Absolutely. But, practically speaking, what happens when Annie makes contact cosmically, as she is doing now, with ideas? What is Martin's task then? Annie, ironically, is in the ideas realm. Although she is able to help others with the business of their lives, she is bringing through ideas from the universal mind now and asking Martin to become the practical one – the leader – in some senses that Annie cannot understand or know about. What is the male task then? Because there are women who can speak to the Earth – many of Annie's clients are 'Earth women'- but what is the male task now?"

"It feels like a rooting process takes place."

"Absolutely. We said the root is shifting. What is happening, Martin?"

"Fresh roots are being placed, I suppose."

"Absolutely. As the man shifts his negative unconscious material he can root mankind even further down than women – even though part of woman's journey has been to descend deeply into the Earth. Men who work on themselves now, will allow mankind to root even more deeply. Does that make sense?

"In other words, although there will be women who can talk about the Earth very skilfully, it is the men will get to it at a deeper level in some ways, and it will be their task to speak Earth-talk, won't it? What does that mean, Martin? How is the Earth receiving mankind now that she is not raging?"

"In a sunnier way, I think."

"Absolutely. Feel down into that deep-rootedness. Feel the way it feels, at this really deep-rooted level now. What is the feeling of the way the Earth will speak to the men, who must be the leaders of men in the future – in Earth consciousness?"

"It feels as though they will just speak it in a very practical way, it will just flow out of them."

"Absolutely. So speak Earth-speak, Martin, in a very practical way. What's the feeling right now that Earth wishes to express to the world, that Annie can't understand, but Martin can?"

"It feels as though there has to be a change in our lifestyle – an acceptance of core issues and values for living our lives. That we can't make assumptions about the resources going on forever. I don't think Earth wants us to be running around like crazy. There's a sense of stillness, of peace on Earth which there hasn't been for a very long time. I think there's a sense of safety on Earth – that this is a place of safety. It is not a threat to walk the Earth."

May we suggest, then, that men will be the purveyors of peaceful, harmonious understanding in some way because their woundedness can manifestly be released, in a way that women's woundedness cannot. In other words, men are protectors and women still need that protection against the feeling that they are not quite safe.

The women are able to bring into consciousness the cosmic dimensions but in some ways their rootedness is not quite so rooted as the men's rootedness now. And in that rootedness by men comes the acknowledgement that mankind is safe; it needn't be warrior-like any more.

The fear of losing territory has, until now, been a male fear and in his new rootedness the man will establish a sense of wonder, not war-likeness at his place on Earth. It will persuade men that they need not be so warrior-like anymore. They can accept the peace that passeth all understanding at the deepest level of their being.

Men will be the workers for harmony and peace because the Earth will establish within herself that harmony and peace, not the depth of rage she felt at the intrusion of the divinity that mankind brought. As men allow the rage of Earth to be released from within themselves, it is they, paradoxically, who will be the harbingers of harmony and peace.

The man will protect the woman, whose sacrifice, if you like, is to sense that her woundedness will never quite be released. So the man still holds the security of the woman in his hand. It is a sacrifice made by the woman in order to be the mediator of cosmic dimensions. The woman will still carry a slight anxiety, an insecurity, that the man will hold in his hand. We feel the way forward, then, is for men to truly release from within themselves the rage and anger of the Earth, in order for them to root deeply into the Earth. They will then lead humanity forward from this place of safety and peace and harmony.

"How does it feel, Martin, for the man to let go all that raging inside, to hold that rooted space for the partnership? So the woman can stay cosmically attuned and be less fearful about her safety?"

"It feels very creative."

"It is terribly creative, isn't it? It is absolutely creative at the root chakra of mankind, which is now so firmly fixed it cannot be unseated."

*   *   *

"May we ask Martin to give us the 'Z' word now. This needs no chapter at all, just the word."

"The word that comes into my mind – I don't know what it means – but it's zenophon."

"It is not in the dictionary, it is a new word. A place of pure balance, integrity and peace."

"And creativity. Delicious creativity. It's the coming together of ... it's the point of focus of Heaven and Earth, or Heaven on Earth."

And So Be It.

also from Rowan Communications

MAKING THE MOST OF THE LIFE YOU'VE GOT

A Manual for the New Millennium

with two audio cassettes

ANNIE WILSON

'Making the Most of the Life You've Got' is a channelled manual for those intent on change; a practical guide that will help readers accept and understand the extraordinary force of energetic change, as we approach the Millennium. Wounds and negative patterning, once acknowledged and released, will give way to the new era, when energy and imagination will be recognised as the building blocks of a life of joyous creativity, celebrating the God within. Annie Wilson offers guidance on money, work, relationships, love-making; and the vital need for a real communication with Nature. Her audio tapes contain simple guided exercises which require only the courage to face life in a new dimension; NOW!

"A simplicity that is moving beyond words."

"A deep experience, different from a normal book."

"I've just done the tape and it's so interesting, relevant, true and releasing."

For workshop information contact the author at
Rowan Communications Ltd.

also from Rowan Communications

THE EVERLASTING RELATIONSHIP

Mother and Child at war and peace

by Tess Nind

The Everlasting Relationship is the changing story of Mother and Child. It is also the author's personal and moving journey in search of eternal truth, contained in the myths of the Moon and its relationship to Earth.

Tess Nind, through her own experience, shows how the tyranny of the child in these difficult times reflects the tyranny within Every Mother. Recognising, understanding and releasing this deep-seated bind can bring about the union of the inner Mother and Child at a profound and creative level.

The Everlasting Relationship offers a new beginning for us all, men and women alike; a fresh approach to Mother and Child as a journey to the Soul, which will be welcomed by all who read this insightful book.

"Magnificent - I gave up the whole day to read it....it was almost an adventure and I had to see the next step. I feel this is what we've been waiting for, I'm deeply impressed".

"It's surprising, shocking, and yet very compelling. It's as if the author has had to undergo these difficult events to find loving energy - and it's not a mental process".

For workshop information contact the author at
Rowan Communications Ltd.